CONTENTS

KHMER
THE LOST EMPIRE OF CAMBODIA

Thierry Zéphir

DISCOVERIES®
HARRY N. ABRAMS, INC., PUBLISHERS

Bordered to the west by the sea, to the north by Thailand and Laos, to the east and the south by Vietnam, Cambodia is far smaller today than it was during its golden age, between the 10th and the 13th century, when Angkor was the capital of the most powerful and opulent empire in Southeast Asia.

CHAPTER 1

LAND AND WATER

The countless reservoirs of Cambodia have always played an essential role in everyday life. In Angkor, the ancient capital, the largest and most beautiful of them were built by the kings. Srah Srang was founded in the 10th century and was renovated in the 12th century by Jayavarman VII, who was also responsible for the lovely landing-stage (opposite) with its balustrades decorated with *nagas*, the mythical cobras with raised heads (right, at Preah Palilay).

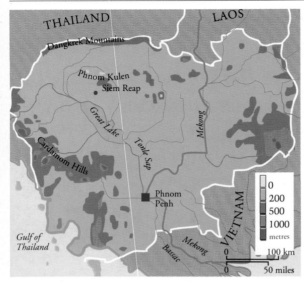

The geography of Cambodia consists of a great plain with the sea in the south, the Mekong in the east and low mountains in the west and the north. Set in the middle of this magnificent natural setting, the Great Lake reflects the alternation between dry and rainy seasons.

The *phnoms*, mountains or hills, seem to have been hammered into the Cambodian plain like nails. Originally they were the chosen sites of temples, but some of them, such as Phnom Chisor, the 'mountain of the sun' (as it is called in the ancient inscriptions) in the southern province of Ta Keo (below), are now occupied by Buddhist monasteries.

Geography

Geographically, the country mainly consists of a vast plain with the low mountain range of the Cardamom Hills in the west and the Dangrek Mountains in the north. The powerful Mekong River crosses Cambodia from north to south as far as Kratie, where it turns westwards to Phnom Penh. From there it once again follows a north–south course, flowing towards

Vietnam, where its majestic waters, exhausted after crossing a fairly flat region, branch out into a number of slow-moving streams that peter out into the South China Sea.

Apart from a few fairly high mountains, such as the Kulen range north-east of Angkor, the perfectly flat expanse of the Cambodian plain is relieved here and there by small hills, known as *phnoms*, which were most probably regarded as sacred from earliest times. With the introduction of Indian culture in the first centuries AD, most of these hills became the seats of the gods, especially the Brahmanist divinities. This tradition has survived up to the present day, although in a different religious context, for nearly every Cambodian *phnom* is crowned with a Buddhist pagoda, in the vicinity or even in place of an earlier sanctuary once dedicated to the gods who came from India, the 'spiritual mother' of Southeast Asia.

Climate

The Cambodian climate is ruled by the monsoons. Indeed, the alternation of dry and humid seasons governs most human activity, giving rhythm to

About 4200 kilometres (2600 miles) long, the Mekong is the seventh longest river in Asia and the fourth largest in terms of volume of flow. It is also the longest river in Southeast Asia. Its source lies in Tibet and its waters, alternately calm or rough depending on the kind of terrain it crosses, flow into a huge delta in the south of Vietnam. The lower Mekong basin irrigates Laos, Cambodia and South Vietnam. Those who live near the river naturally benefit from it, despite the occasional disastrous floods.

everyday life. From November to May, the dry season gradually makes everyone and everything sluggish in an increasingly oppressive heat, which is at its most stifling in the months of March and April. From June to October, the rainy season brings new life, with irregular rainfall that becomes very heavy during the

The Khmer people, with their houses built on stilts or afloat on the water, adapted their way of life to the changing water levels.

last two months; in Phnom Penh this annual renaissance is celebrated every November by the Festival of the Waters, which marks the moment when the waters begin to subside.

The rise of the waters

One of the most remarkable geo-ecological features of Cambodia is the existence, almost in the centre of the plain, of a vast lake, which quadruples in size during the rainy season.

From June on, the waters of the lake begin to rise, because of the combined effect of the natural flow of the rivers, the rains and the waters of the Mekong, which is itself swollen by the snows that melt in the summer in Tibet, where it has its source. Then the floods from the powerful river produce a curious and unusual effect: they reverse the normal course of the Tonle Sap, the southern outlet of the Great Lake, and

The changing water levels have given rise to a ritual inherited from ancient Khmer tradition. 'It is marvellous to see the hundred pirogues (there used to be five hundred) advance like an attacking army, giving the impression from afar, with their cheerful paddlers standing upright, of a galloping cavalry passing like a gust of wind, saluted by the cries of the joyful populace' (Adhémard Leclère, *Cambodge: Fêtes Civiles et Religieuses*, 1916).

turn the flow of the water in the opposite direction. At that point the surface area of this inland soft-water lake increases from 3000 to 10,000 square kilometres (from 1800 to 6200 square miles). Its waters form a perfect breeding ground for fish and these extremely favourable conditions were no doubt one of the main reasons why Angkor, the capital, was founded on the northern bank, at the edge of the flood area, out of reach of the high waters and yet close enough to an inexhaustible source of food.

Water mythology: *naga* the snake

Today, as in the past, water remains crucial to Khmer life. The Cambodians, like everyone else, are dependent for survival on a constant source of water, which is used to quench thirst, cook food and irrigate and cultivate the land. Every home in the Cambodian countryside has its own pool or *trapeang*, which fills up and dries out according to the seasons.

However, in ancient Cambodia the beneficial and vital role of water went far beyond the practical aspects of daily life. In local mythological traditions it was symbolized by a snake or *naga*. This mythical animal, a many-headed cobra, derived from Indian cultural models that were adapted by the various Southeast Asian peoples.

From time immemorial it has been associated with water and with the purely material wealth that water provided and guaranteed. So this animal became linked with prosperity and the image of the snake guarding a treasure in its underground domain soon became established.

The *naga*, a many-headed cobra symbolizing water, is found on nearly every monument (background, from the temple of Preah Palilay in Angkor). Unreal, haughty and frightening, the 12th-century *nagas* (like this bronze sculpture from Banteay Srei, left) are among the most beautiful works of Khmer sculpture.

Legendary origins

One day a Brahman of Indian origin, a certain Kaundinya, married a local snake-princess, the *nagi* Soma. This legend, which situates the origin of one of the most ancient royal lines in Cambodia, the monarchs of Funan, between the 'civilized' (Indian Brahman) and the 'non-civilized' (local princess), can be interpreted as a distorted image, as the unconscious memory of a historical event dating to the first contacts between the Indian and Khmer people. Those who came from the world of water or formed part of it were conquered peacefully and then organized by 'foreigners'. Yet it is important to remember that although these 'foreigners' managed to establish some of their own traditions in a new country on a permanent basis, it was only because the host country was culturally receptive to them.

A part from fishing, rice-growing was probably the most important activity from earliest times in Cambodia. Here, as in most other parts of Southeast Asia, flooded rice fields (opposite far right) are a very common sight. After being sown and growing for a month or a month and a half in fields used as seed-beds, the rice is planted out in the flooded paddy fields and ripens about three months later. With good irrigation practices, it is theoretically possible to grow three crops a year.

The Khmer hydraulic system

Apart from the legends and imagery of ancient Cambodia, a number of inscriptions from that time contain specific references to water. Countless dykes, reservoirs, drainage and other systems are mentioned in inscriptions not only for their practical use but also for their religious significance.

The normal method of cultivating rice in terraces in the

north of the country and the drainage systems needed for growing anything at all in the delta area were followed by the first type of well-thought-out rural development: a system of carefully positioned dykes to contain the streams of water and then redistribute them across sloping ground.

Indeed, the power of Angkor between the 9th and the 13th century largely rested on this careful management of water.

This embryonic irrigation technique seems to have been mastered from the 6th century. It can be compared with the development of religious

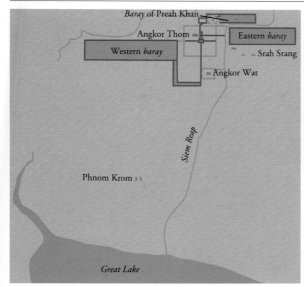

Baray of Preah Khan

Angkor Thom

Western *baray*

Eastern *baray*

Srah Srang

Angkor Wat

Siem Reap

Phnom Krom

Great Lake

architecture in durable materials (mainly bricks) and the establishment of a basic town-planning system, reflecting the growing power of the various pre-Angkor kingdoms.

The period of the *barays*

The next stage, full mastery of hydraulic engineering and large-scale irrigation projects, involved the construction of *barays*, both in the capital and on other sites. These are not exactly lakes but vast reservoirs using four-sided strong dykes, which sometimes spanned a very large area.

Besides the *barays*, which were filled by rainwater and above all by rivers whose course was sometimes diverted for that purpose, the hydraulic system of Angkor consisted of a large number of canals used to water the paddy fields and to fill the moats round the sanctuaries.

Water played an important part in both economic and religious life. Indeed it has been suggested that a *baray*, the centre of which was always the site of a

The topography of the site of Angkor is known from observations made in the field since the mid-19th century, from aerial photographs (above) taken in the 1930s by Victor Goloubew and, finally, from satellite pictures (opposite). They reveal the basis of the Angkor hydraulic system with its canals, reservoirs and moats, which are clearly visible on the satellite photos, as is the border between the areas that may become flooded during the annual swelling of the Great Lake and the areas that are constantly flooded. The *barays* work very simply: they fill with rain or river water after which, depending on the natural slope of the land, the waters are rechannelled into the rice fields by a system of primary and secondary canals (plan, above left).

temple, was only regarded as being effective because of its close association with the spiritual world. In practice, however, the system was not nearly as efficient as it was supposed to be: these immense reservoirs rapidly began to silt up and therefore became less productive, if not useless, unless they were cleaned out. However, there is no evidence that this ever occurred at Angkor.

The large number of *barays* on the site of Angkor bears witness not so much to an increase in the cultivation of the land or to a rise in the population as to the limits of the system: in short, once one *baray* had dried up, another had to be constructed. Obviously it did not dry up overnight and the process took some years.

The success of the various kings who succeeded to the throne of Angkor was due mainly to their ability to manage their 'hydraulic estate' with wisdom and foresight and, where necessary, to have a new *baray* built before the water reserves became too low, while making utmost use of the older lakes, depending on their location.

Barrage-bridges

Farming, mainly rice growing, was the main means of subsistence for a population that was certainly large in the golden age of Angkor (even if it is impossible to give any accurate figures). Although no information exists on the system of farming at the time – either intensive with several crops a year over a fairly small area or extensive with a single annual crop over a large area – we do know that the economic system as a whole in Angkor was based largely on the use of irrigation techniques.

E very large reservoir in Angkor has a little island with a sanctuary reflecting its sacred nature, like the temple of the West Mebon in the middle of the western *baray*, 8 kilometres (nearly 5 miles) long by 2.2 kilometres (about 1½ miles) wide, built in the 11th century (above). Bas-reliefs show that these reservoirs were very common. Below: lotus flowers emerge from the reservoir.

If the system failed, then the very survival of the empire could be at stake. One of the reasons for the weakening of central power after the reign of Jayavarman VII (1181–1218?) was precisely the change in, and breakdown of, the system of water distribution and the problems of maintaining it.

A combination of unfavourable political and human factors seems to have led Khmer engineers to alter their approach to irrigation totally in the course of the 13th century. They stopped building the gigantic *barays*, which were so difficult to maintain, and started putting simple barrage-bridges across rivers. Various structures of this kind have been identified and studied, including the highly

The laterite bridge of Kompong Kdei, known as Spean Praptos, is one of the most impressive of the Khmer barrage-bridges. It dates from the first half of the 13th century and is 87 metres (285 feet) long. The arches are very narrow because of the method of construction by a system of corbels. The architect Jacques Dumarçay has shown how these arches could be fully or partially closed in order to contain the water

impressive Spean Praptos near Kompong Kdei.

This new approach was one of the many changes that seemed to lead to the gradual decline of the Khmer Empire. Water was no longer collected and redistributed under central control. Instead it became the prerogative of the owner of the land traversed by a river on which a barrage-bridge was situated. Both feudal landowners and small potentates became increasingly powerful in the course of history.

upriver from the bridge. This method of irrigation, where a noria was needed to contain the water subsequently used to irrigate the surrounding fields, was very different from the *baray* system.

'**I**n the first century AD a kingdom was established in the lowland valley of the Mekong, known until then by the Chinese name Funan.... The kingdom of Cambodia, sometimes called the 'Khmer Empire', is geographically and ... also historically the successor, the continuation of Funan on the Indochinese peninsula.'

George Coedès
Les Peuples de la péninsule indochinoise, 1962

CHAPTER 2

THE BEGINNINGS OF THE KHMER WORLD

The classical representation of the Buddha (opposite) as serene and meditative (with half-closed eyes, a gentle smile, regular features and the cranial protuberance that was one of the characteristic marks of the 'great man') became widespread in Southeast Asia from the first centuries AD. Right: the bull Nandin, Shiva's mount, derives from Brahmanist tradition.

The early history of the Khmer, from the first centuries of the Christian era until the beginning of the 9th century, is known as the pre-Angkor period. It came to an end when Jayavarman II proclaimed himself *chakravartin* ('holder of the wheel'), a term designating a universal ruler in Indian tradition, and was crowned king of the Khmer kings in the year 802 on the mountain of Mahendraparvata, the present Phnom Kulen.

The early pre-Angkor period: Funan

It was probably during the first or second century AD that India started to establish contact with neighbouring countries throughout Southeast Asia. Indian navigators set sail in search of new lands, dreaming of the fabulous riches that Southeast Asia seemed to offer at the time. These expeditions, whose purpose was not colonization but peaceful trade, led to the establishment and incorporation of elements of Indian culture in the 'Indianized states', such as the Indonesian islands and the delta regions of the Irrawaddy, the Menam and the Mekong.

In the southern part of continental Southeast Asia, this was the age of the kings of Funan, who settled on the lower and middle reaches of the Mekong. It could be described as a kind of Indianized maritime empire involved in transcontinental trade that extended to China and India on the one hand (various objects from these two countries, but mainly from India, have been discovered in Oc Eo in South Vietnam) and the Roman Empire on the other

Although its exact provenance is unknown, the carnelian capricorn (fish-goat) intaglio shown above probably dates back to the Funan period. Many foreign objects from then were discovered in Oc Eo (Vietnam).

The Sanskrit stele of Vo Canh (left) discovered in Champa, in what is now Vietnam, is the earliest (second half of the 3rd century) inscription to reflect the spread of Indian culture throughout Southeast Asia.

(several intaglios, coins with an effigy of Antoninus Pius dated 152).

Neither architecture nor sculpture has survived from that period, apart from substructures of buildings that are impossible to date. This absence suggests that both were made of organic, perishable materials. However, some interesting tin objects point to the fact that metalwork may have been a typical product of the Mekong delta area.

Accounts by Chinese travellers, many of which are preserved in embassy records incorporated in various dynastic annals of imperial China, provide useful information on ancient Cambodia. The earliest of these is by Kang Tai and Zhu Ying, two envoys of the Wu emperor, and dates to the mid-3rd century AD. The original is lost but fragments can be found in later annals. The kingdom of Funan is described thus: 'The kingdom of Funan is more than 3000 li [where 1 li is equivalent to 540 metres or 590 yards] west of Linyi [this is Champa, an important Indianized kingdom that has now disappeared but was originally situated in the centre and south of what is now Vietnam. Throughout their history the Khmer had many contacts, including wars, with this kingdom], in a large bay of the sea.... There are walled towns, palaces and dwelling houses. The men ... practise farming.... They like to engrave ornaments and to carve.... They have books and keep archives.... The characters of their writing resemble those of the Hou [a people of Central Asia whose writing, like that of Cambodia, derives from certain Indian alphabets].'

The last king of Funan, Rudravarman, is not mentioned after about AD 550 and soon after that the name Funan disappeared. It was replaced in Chinese sources by Zhenla.

Many intaglios of Indian or Mediterranean origin have been found on the site of Oc Eo (above). They must have reached Cambodia via the overseas trade between Southeast Asia and China or India on the one hand and, beyond it, the Roman world on the other.

Metalwork in tin is very characteristic of the Oc Eo site, as shown by this amulet (below), probably made locally.

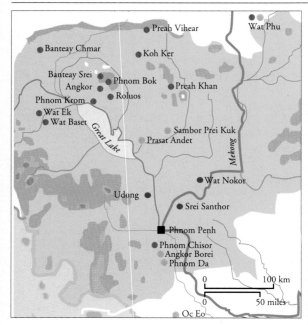

Pre-Angkor sites

Angkor sites

Post-Angkor sites

Angkor is the best-known site in Cambodia. Yet the ancient Khmer Empire included numerous other sites ranging from simple mounds, the only remaining traces of ancient brick sanctuaries, to temple complexes forming entire cities, such as Koh Ker in northern Cambodia (second quarter of the 10th century). An inventory of all the Khmer sites drawn up by Etienne-Edmond Lunet de Lajonquière was published early this century and work on it is still continuing. Although it is in many respects dated, it remains an essential and irreplaceable working tool now that a number of the sites it describes have disappeared or become inaccessible.

Wat Phu (opposite), dedicated to Bhadreshvara (one of the names of Shiva) in what is now Laos, was a holy site not only for the Khmer, but also for their neighbours the Chams, from early times. Most of the remains date back to the 11th and 12th centuries.

Zhenla: the ancestor of Cambodia

A 10th-century inscription tells the dynastic legend attached to the kingdom of Zhenla which, although different from that of the kingdom of Funan, is also inspired by an Indian legend: the god Shiva himself gave a hermit called Kambu Svayambhuva, the eponymous ancestor of the inhabitants of Kambujadesha (our modern 'Cambodia'), the hand in marriage of a celestial nymph, the beautiful Mera. The union of Kambu and Mera, whose merged names probably explain the origin of the term 'Khmer', produced a line of kings from which the Angkor sovereigns later claimed descent (although they continued to refer also to the mythical union of the Funan Kaundinya and Soma).

The cradle of Zhenla lay in the region of Wat Phu, in the south of what is now Laos. Epigraphic evidence testifies to the existence of a capital, Bhavapura,

founded in the second half of the 6th century by King Bhavavarman I, a prince of Funan who married a princess from the royal family of Zhenla and thus became the ruler of that kingdom. Although the site has not yet been identified, it is probably somewhere east of the Great Lake, in the province of Kompong Thom.

The 7th and 8th centuries: the truth behind the legend

From the 7th century the sites and the sculptures that have been discovered give a more precise, although still fragmentary, picture of the pre-Angkor Khmer country.

In the south, the site of Angkor Borei and more generally the region around it, once regarded as a capital of Funan, perhaps the last one,

Harihara is a combined image of two gods, Vishnu (Hari, on the left side of the statue) and Shiva (Hara, on the right side), each character- ized by his attributes, headdress and clothing. Like many other pre- Angkor statues with several arms, this Harihara (7th century, from the temple of Asram Maha Rosei) had a supporting stone arch that originally went down to the base of the statue and linked the arms to one another and the upper hands to the head in order to make the work more stable.

The decoration on the temples of Sambor Prei Kuk (7–9th century) consists mainly of bas-reliefs, known as 'flying palaces' because they were thought to represent the heavenly abode of the divinities (left).

This statue of Durga, one of the manifestations of the wife of the god Shiva, from Sambor Prei Kuk is one of the loveliest pre-Angkor sculptures. It dates from the 7th century. Modelled with great sensitivity and faithfulness to nature, the form of this young woman is a perfect expression of the feminine energy the goddess was supposed to embody.

was certainly the centre of an important kingdom. (Angkor means 'royal city', from the Sanskrit *nagara*, and Borei 'holy city', from the Sanskrit *puri*.) It has left some monuments and a remarkable body of sculpture, which includes some of the great masterpieces of Khmer art. Excavations now under way will probably provide more information on its history.

Large complexes of religious monuments that can be dated more accurately are also known further north, like those in Sambor Prei Kuk.

One of the successors of Bhavavarman I, Ishanavarman I, was responsible for some of the oldest temples on this site: the southern group (which includes three temples) is attributed to him. We know from inscriptions that this king established a vast kingdom, virtually covering the territory of present-day Cambodia. One of his descendants, Jayavarman I, still ruled a large kingdom in the second half of the 7th century. During the 8th century it appears that this territory was split into two parts: land Zhenla (in a mountainous northern region) and water Zhenla (in the south, bordered by the sea and the lakes). This division of Zhenla probably accompanied the fragmentation of power between various kingdoms of different sizes and strengths.

Several monuments now in a state of ruin (for example Prasat Prei Kmeng) testify to the fact that the Khmer began to settle in the western part of Angkor in the 7th century. Prasat Ak Yum, the first temple-mountain on this site, dates to that period of settlement (7–8th century).

This famous Buddha (c. 6th century) discovered in Dong Duong (Vietnam) was an Indian or Singhalese import. Similar images have been found elsewhere in Southeast Asia but not in Cambodia.

Indian influence in Southeast Asia

India's main contribution to Southeast Asia is its language, Sanskrit, and the religions that were its predominant means of expression.

The first archaeological and historical evidence for the spread of religions originating in India to Southeast Asia is in the form of inscriptions and bronze images of the Buddha. Discovered all along the trade routes that crisscrossed the region, most of these works, when not imported, reflect Indian or Singhalese styles but do not date much further back than the 5th or 6th century.

The fact that the earliest images are Buddhist does not necessarily mean that Buddhism was the first religion to reach the shores of Southeast Asia. It is believed that the religion founded at the turn of the 6th and 5th century BC in northern India by the sage of the Shakya clan (Shakyamuni), called the Buddha or the 'Enlightened One', became established or was adopted at the same time as Brahmanism, the legacy of the ancient Vedic tradition, during the first centuries AD.

In the course of the second half of the 2nd millennium BC, India, or at least the entire northern part of it, became the home of various groups of nomadic peoples known as the Aryans. They brought with them a specific way of thinking, a type of social organization – which was to develop in the subcontinent and eventually produce the caste system – a language (an archaic form of Sanskrit) and a body of sacred texts originally handed down orally: the *Vedas*, meaning 'knowledge'. These texts form the spiritual foundation of classical India. They became established in India side by side with pre-existing animist and chthonic cults.

In Khmer art Indra, the Vedic king of the gods, is usually shown astride his mount, the three-headed elephant Airavata. The sculpture above is from Banteay Srei.

Varuna, one of the most important gods of Vedism, plays a secondary role in Brahmanism. One of the *dikpalakas* (guardians of the four cardinal and four intermediate points of the compass), he is the guardian of the west. Khmer iconography often represents him on a *hamsa* (wild duck or goose). Left: a rare statue of Varuna dating from the 10th century.

The Vedic religion is essentially ritualistic and is focused on gods who represent the forces of nature: the waters (of the earth or heaven), the sun, the wind. Within this rich pantheon – which already included most of the main gods of Hinduism – a marked trend towards monotheism was reflected in the belief in a universal soul, a creator. The internal development of this religious system was based on the idea of cyclical time, rebirth (*samsara*) and retribution for deeds (the famous *karma* that weighs so heavily on the individual soul). The tendency towards ritual remained and in the 6th century BC various heresies that offered a different road to salvation (that is, a means of escaping the 'infernal' cycle of reincarnation) began to appear: Jainism and, rather more important because of the way it developed within and outside India, Buddhism.

Different religions coexist happily

After spreading throughout Southeast Asia, Brahmanism (or Hinduism) and Buddhism developed side by side. They lived with very ancient chthonic cults which they did not try to destroy and with which they had to become reconciled; in fact they have left many traces from early times until today.

As is the case in India, the two systems seem to have laid more emphasis on their common features than on their differences. One of the notable aspects of the Indian religions in Cambodia lies in their harmonious coexistence, sometimes verging on syncretism, which is reflected again and again in both

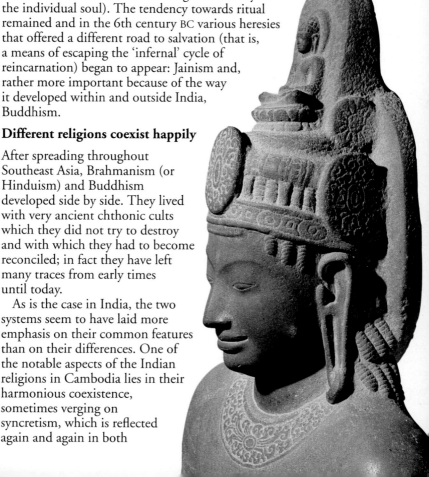

Lokeshvara (below) is the most frequently represented of the Bodhisattvas, those compassionate beings who have delayed entering *nirvana* in order to help other souls search for salvation.

inscriptions and monuments. It is remarkable how the devotees, both the followers of Buddha and the zealous supporters of Shiva and Vishnu, faithfully and carefully learned the teachings of India and perpetuated and at times transcended them. This strict faith did not result in any kind of paralysis and, once they had taken root, the Indian religions evolved to produce fruits unknown in their mother country. This can be seen from the image on the right, astonishingly faithful to the letter – namely a Buddhist text, the *Karandavyuhasutra* – and yet unique in the Indianized world: radiating Lokeshvara as a cosmic being.

Buddhas and Brahmanist divinities

From the pre-Angkor age, Buddhism and Brahmanism seem to have shared the favours of those who commissioned the works and therefore of the sculptors fairly equitably.

The Buddha is represented in the same way as in India, as are the Bodhisattvas, those divine beings characteristic of the 'developed' form of Buddhism known as Mahayana, who delay the moment of their own 'liberation' to help others on their way, thereby gaining compassion and wisdom. The Vaishnavite pantheon is remarkably rich: Vishnu himself in his main aspect, but also in some of his manifestations or avatars – in Sanskrit *avatara* literally means a 'descent'. The iconography of

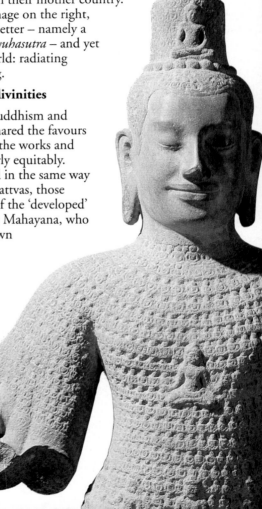

The Lokeshvara with radiating arms (below) is a cosmic image expressing the universal compassion of the Bodhisattva. An effigy of the Buddha comes out of every pore.

The image of the meditating Buddha protected by a *naga* (left) first appeared in Cambodia towards the end of the 10th century, after which it became more common. On this work, dating from the early 13th century, the *naga's* lower body and upper heads are missing.

The Khmer *linga*, a phallic representation of Shiva (below), consists of a cubic base symbolizing Brahma (the creator), an octagonal middle section symbolizing Vishnu (the preserver) and a circular upper section symbolizing Rudra, an aspect of Shiva (the destroyer).

Shivaism, the other major trend of Brahmanism, which was almost always the state religion of the Angkor period (apart from a few exceptions), is equally rich. Shiva himself is most frequently represented in the form of the *linga*, the symbol of his creative power.

The Shiva of Phnom Bok (above) displays some of the iconographic characteristics of the anthropomorphous representation of the god: the third eye on the forehead (the eye of knowledge), ascetic chignon of braided hair, crescent moon on the cylindrical headdress. The figure of Ardhanarishvara, the androgynous form of Shiva, reflects the god's unity in diversity. This iconography is unusual in Khmer art. Left: an exceptional image from the early 13th century.

Each of the great Brahmanist divinities has a 'family'. Shiva is the husband of Parvati, who also takes on many different aspects: Uma (the light), Kali (the dark) and Durga (the inaccessible). Left: on a bas-relief from Banteay Samre, the goddess Durga – who is in fact the manifestation of the feminine energy (*shakti*) of all the gods – is destroying a demon in the form of a buffalo. Ganesha (below left), the god with an elephant's head associated with greed and knowledge, was regarded as the son of Shiva and Parvati, as was Skanda (below right), the god of war, shown riding a peacock.

Vishnu, like Shiva, could assume various forms. Some of his avatars or manifestations appear in epic myths: Rama or Krishna (opposite above, fighting the *naga* Kaliya on an 11th-century lintel). He can also appear in other part-human, part-animal manifestations, such as Kurma (the tortoise) or Narasimha (the man-lion). Yet he is most frequently depicted in his four-armed form as *chaturbhuja*. Wearing a headdress in the form of a cylindrical tiara, the god (left, a 9th-century work) has four arms and carries the most characteristic of his attributes: a small globe (the earth), a disc (a throwing weapon but also a symbol of the sun), a conch (symbol of the links between the god and the ocean) and a club (a weapon but also a symbol of sovereign power).

Brahma, the creator of the cosmos whose four mouths are said to have uttered the four *Vedas* (below right), is a god who is rarely depicted despite his importance. In the Brahmanist triad, *trimurti* or the threefold form of the divine, he is the creator, while Shiva is the destroyer and Vishnu the preserver. Below left: a pre-Angkor stele on which the gods are represented only by their attributes.

State centralism gradually became established in Angkor from the early 9th century. Supported by the faithful, at the head of a complex social pyramid comprising a large and unwieldy administration, every ruler seems to have been intent on finding a place in history by instituting public works for the common good and building magnificent temples to the glory of the gods.

CHAPTER 3

THE FIRST KINGS OF ANGKOR

The temple of Baksei Chamkrong (opposite) looms out of the forest like an apparition. After Angkor was abandoned as the capital in the mid-15th century, nature took over and radically changed the aspect of the site. Left: a 12th-century 'library' in Banteay Samre.

From the 11th century the sacred nature of the rivers flowing from Phnom Kulen to irrigate Angkor was reflected in reliefs on the adjacent rocks, mainly representing *lingas*. They emphasize the assimilation of rivers such as Kbal Spean (left) with the Ganga (Ganges), the holy river of India.

Jayavarman II: the founder of the Khmer Empire

The career of the future Jayavarman II, regarded as the founder of the Angkorean kingship, began towards 790. Around that year this ambitious prince, who left no inscriptions from his own time but is well known from others dating from after his reign, set about freeing his country from foreign rule, an Indonesian kingdom, that of the Java people, where he is said to have spent some time in exile. This religious and political liberation was celebrated on Phnom Kulen, a chain of hills north of the Great Lake, in 802, the year associated with the beginning of the Angkor period, though the main

The only statues in the round from Phnom Kulen are the images of the god Vishnu with four arms and a smooth, cylindrical headdress in the form of a mitre. These works dating from the 9th century form a stylistic link between the pre-Angkor and Angkor periods. The Vishnu (left) discovered near Rup Arak still bears traces between the arm and the head of the supporting arch that gave pre-Angkor works their stability.

temple of the first Angkor, Phnom Bakheng, was not built for another century, under Yashovarman I. From 802 to 1431 Angkor was the symbol of the Khmer Empire.

The reign of Jayavarman II was marked by activity – he united a number of kingdoms and domains under his rule, founded or developed several cities and ordered various temples to be built on Phnom Kulen. He is said to have died in Hariharalaya (near the present village of Roluos) soon after 830. Little is known about his son and successor, Jayavarman III (830?–after 860), except that he was a Vaishnavite and that his reign must have been uneventful. That may not be a point of great interest in itself, yet it does indicate the stability, perhaps even peace, enjoyed by the newly created empire.

Inscriptions are fundamental to our knowledge of Khmer civilization

Though little is known about the matter, it seems that the Khmer were interested in preserving their immediate past. Yet, if the royal chronicles, which are fairly recent since the earliest versions were written in the early 19th century, do indeed refer to the past, it is either a legendary one or a recent past, of which they give an embellished or distorted account.

Nothing remains of ancient Cambodian manuscript literature; it consisted of not only

Among the Phnom Kulen monuments, Prasat Damrei Krap stands out for its similarities, in terms of composition and decoration, with the contemporary architecture of the neighbouring kingdom of Champa: twin pilasters on the corners of the lower part of the *prasats* and false terraces; arches with volutes above the niches.

Ancient Cambodian inscriptions typically begin with an invocation to the gods, sometimes followed by the genealogy of the donor and a list of his works, often in the form of a lengthy eulogy. This shows the religious and historical importance of these texts and also explains why everyday Khmer life did not feature in them at all. The inscription at Baksei Chamkrong (left, 948) is a good example.

In 16th-century inscriptions, as in this one in Angkor Wat (below), the form of the letters is plainer and less regular. Changes in calligraphy help to date these inscriptions.

religious texts but also administrative, commercial and other documents, written on leaves (or perhaps on paper that the Khmer could have obtained from China, thanks to the trade relations between the two countries at that time). A fleeting glimpse of these 'books' can be seen in the narrative bas-reliefs on the temple of Angkor Wat and the carved monuments of the Bayon. With the earliest manuscripts lost for ever and the most recent texts proving to be fairly unreliable historically, it is only inscriptions that can help to trace Khmer history.

Cambodian inscriptions are closely linked to religious life. With very few exceptions, all the inscriptions that have been found were cut into the stone to commemorate a religious foundation, which explains why they are difficult to use in historical research.

Three languages have been identified, using the same script derived from a southern Indian model. Pali, an Indo-Aryan language, was only used very occasionally until the 14th century, after which Theravada Buddhism, mainly if not exclusively expressed through Pali in Cambodia, became the dominant Cambodian religion, which it has remained until now.

Most of the early texts (until the 14th century) that have survived are written in Sanskrit, another Indo-Aryan language, and in Khmer, which stems from an entirely different language, Mon-Khmer. The inscriptions, of very variable length, were often in two languages. In such a case the first section, which could perhaps be described as the official part, was usually written in Sanskrit.

Monuments and great works: witnesses to history

Since the documents used to study Khmer history tend to come from a religious context, on the whole very little is known about the day-to-day

Pre-Angkor script closely resembles South Indian writing, from which it stems. The stele of Tuol Neak Ta Bak Ka (c. 7th century), written in ancient Khmer and adorned with an image of the bull Nandin, specifies the quantity of salt to be delivered to certain sanctuaries.

There is a wealth of stucco decoration on the brick masonry of the temple of Preah Ko (879). The male and female figures on either side of the doors and blind doors are sculpted from sandstone monoliths, as are the frames. The little columns supporting the lintel are octagonal, a shape characteristic of the Angkor period.

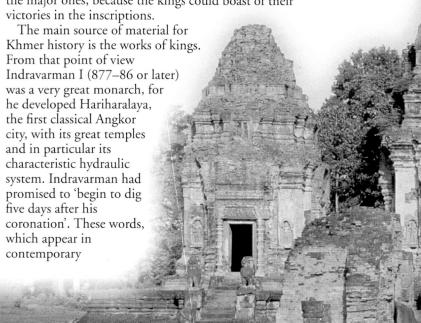

events of life during the Angkor period. More information is available on wars, but even then only the major ones, because the kings could boast of their victories in the inscriptions.

The main source of material for Khmer history is the works of kings. From that point of view Indravarman I (877–86 or later) was a very great monarch, for he developed Hariharalaya, the first classical Angkor city, with its great temples and in particular its characteristic hydraulic system. Indravarman had promised to 'begin to dig five days after his coronation'. These words, which appear in contemporary inscriptions, presumably relate to the construction of the dykes of the Indratataka or the *baray* of Roluos, the first large reservoir in the Angkor region. The king's achievements thus began with a great public work. To the south of this enormous lake measuring 3800 × 800 metres (2½ × ½ miles), the king set up the statues of the divinities of Preah Ko in 879, dedicated to some of his predecessors on the throne who thus became protectors of the realm. Finally, in 881, he built the first well-preserved temple-mountain in the Angkor region: Bakong, a five-tiered artificial pyramid, the seat of a *linga* named Indreshvara, a reference to one of the names commonly given to the god Shiva, Ishvara, and the king's own name, Indravarman, in accordance with a custom that was to be repeated frequently.

The retaining wall of the uppermost terrace of the pyramid of Bakong (881) contains the earliest narrative bas-relief known to date. Only a few details remain visible (below).

The six sanctuaries of the temple of Preah Ko opening towards the east and arranged in two rows of three on a north to south axis were built of brick. The three towers in the eastern row housed images of Shiva, the towers in the western row (not visible on the photograph, left) contained images of his wife, the goddess. These statues were erected by Indravarman I for the 'spiritual benefit' of some of his ancestors and predecessors on the throne. The three images of Nandin in front of the sanctuaries have given the temple its modern name of Preah Ko, the 'sacred bull'.

Architectural features such as lintels – left, on the temple of Lolei (893) – are a means of dating temples accurately.

The Bakheng style is cold and geo-metrical, as shown by this image (below), unusual in the Angkor period, of the god Harihara, half Vishnu, half Shiva.

Yashovarman I and the 109 towers of Bakheng

Majestic works for which Yashovarman I (889–early 10th century) was responsible include the temple of Lolei (893) built on a little artificial island on the *baray* of Roluos, the Yashodharatataka or eastern *baray* of Angkor (over 7 kilometres, or 4 miles, east to west and almost 2 kilometres, 1 mile, north to south), the first Yashodharapura (the first city of Angkor), the temple-mountain of Phnom Bakheng, the temples of Phnom Bok and Phnom Krom, together with a very large number of monasteries, of which some of the foundation steles have been found. Although many are now in ruins or have even disappeared, they all attest to the greatness and munificence of their founder, the great Yashovarman I.

The next two reigns were less prolific, although some splendid monuments were built (in fact, building work continued in Angkor for most of the time up until the end of Jayavarman VII's reign in the early 13th century). They include the very beautiful temple of Baksei Chamkrong built under Harshavarman I and the remarkable Prasat Kravan, a Vaishnavite monument erected by dignitaries and consecrated in 921, whose originality lies in the bas-reliefs in two of its five brick towers.

The Khmer temple

As the earthly dwelling of the divinity to whom it is dedicated, the Khmer temple in its layout and

The small Shivaist temple-mountain of Baksei Chamkrong was founded by Harshavarman I in the first quarter of the 10th century. In 948, the date of the inscription on the jambs of the sanctuary door, Rajendravarman

symbolism obeys the strict rules set out in religious treatises well known in India but of which not a single example has been found from ancient Cambodia. The choice of site for building a temple, the direction it faces, its dimensions and date of consecration were all based on surveys carried out beforehand by the monks, the architects and those who commissioned it. Only a monument that met the religious requirements was worthy of receiving the statue of a deity.

The Khmer temple, like the Indian temple, aspired

made a new foundation here and renovated the tower-sanctuary. The temple was intended as an image of Kailasa, the mythical mountain and abode of the god Shiva. It is well proportioned, with gradually reducing terraces and narrowing steps, accentuating the effect of height.

Prasat Kravan (921) is one of the only temples containing bas-reliefs inside the sanctuary. The large, well-preserved and finely sculpted compositions carved in the brickwork represent various gods. Left: Vishnu on his mount Garuda (north wall, right of the entrance). Below left: Vishnu Trivikrama, the god of the 'three steps' who reconquers the worlds on a demon that had oppressed them (south wall, left of the entrance). The west wall at the back of the sanctuary also contains a majestic representation of the eight-armed Vishnu, surrounded by numerous little figures in attitudes of homage, their hands joined at breast level or above their heads. The northern tower also contains represent-ations of Lakshmi, Vishnu's consort (opposite).

The terraced pyramids of the temple-mountains are all artificial except for Phnom Bakheng. The five terraces of the large uncompleted temple of Ta Keo (left) reach a height of 22 metres (c. 72 feet), while the base measures c. 120 metres (c. 393 feet) east to west by 100 metres (c. 328 feet) north to south.

The temple-mountains of Angkor all differ. From Pre Rup (below left) to Ta Keo, which is a later structure (below right), the number of added structures (long halls, *prasats*) decreases. In Ta Keo a continuous gallery was constructed on the second terrace, while no such structure existed at Pre Rup. Although the composition of the summit remained unchanged (a quincunx of tower-sanctuaries), the plan of the *prasats* was enlarged in Ta Keo by adding porches.

to be the terrestrial image of the deity's heavenly abode: Khmer architecture reflects a lively dialectic between macrocosm and microcosm.

Structure of the temple

The core of a Khmer temple generally consists of one or more tower-sanctuaries, the *prasat*, on a square ground plan, although there are exceptions like the octagonal and rectangular monuments of the pre-Angkor site of Sambor Prei Kuk (7th century).

The design of the classical tower-sanctuary is absolutely symmetrical: there is one real doorway (generally facing east), with three blind doorways on

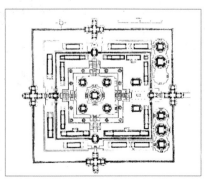
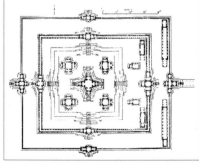

the other three sides. From the 10th century a rectangular anteroom directly adjacent to the entrance doorway could be added to this very simple basic pattern.

The entire development of the Khmer *prasat* starts from this basic structure, with the addition of porches and superstructures, sometimes double, on every facade of the building. Much the same applies to the development of some of the surrounding buildings, such as the pseudo-libraries and *gopuras* (the access gates to the enclosures). The transformation of the rectangular chambers into continuous galleries in the course of the 10th century and later on the changes to the roofing of these galleries – the transition from a wooden roof covered in tiles to a corbelled sandstone vault – can be traced to attempts to make the structures look lighter and to enhance the formal beauty of these monuments.

Above the substructure the Khmer *prasat* takes the form of a tower, which, starting from the bottom, comprises: a moulded plinth, the main body of the building, a cornice and several levels rising in decreasing stages in imitation of a tiered structure. The forms

This miniature version of a *prasat* comes from the temple of Banteay Srei. These scale models of the real tower-sanctuaries were used as antefixas, architectural elements, on the corners of each of the four false storeys.

gradually reduce in size repeating those of the lower part of the building. The whole monument is crowned by a circular ornament in the form of a lotus flower or a pot-bellied vase.

Materials

When they were completed, which was not always the case, the Khmer monuments were decorated mainly round the doorway and the blind doorways. It is a double system, made up, firstly, of a pediment supported at either end by a pillar and, secondly, of a lintel supported on either end by a small column. It is these decorative features in particular that help to date the monuments fairly accurately.

In general, the pre-Angkor master-builders used bricks, often faced in stucco or limestone mortar, while the Angkor builders tended to use sandstone, either for the decorative features or for the main structure, and laterite for the foundations and the less important parts of the architectural complex.

The wood is very poorly preserved and virtually none survives from periods before the 19th century. Yet it was widely used at all times and all domestic buildings were constructed in wood, which explains why they have totally disappeared. However, even in buildings constructed of durable materials – such as religious architecture, which was designed to last for ever since it was intended for eternal beings, the divinities – wood was also used, sometimes indeed wrongly, as is the case of the beams set in stone lintels

The doorways were surrounded by a double frame: the internal 'frame' is made up of two small columns supporting a lintel, the external 'frame' of two pilasters supporting the outer edges of the pediment. The most common form is an undulating frame with many foliate shapes, as in the northern 'library' of Banteay Srei (above), but triangular examples are also found.

The three noble materials were used at Pre Rup (opposite).

that were shaped for that purpose. It is self-evident that buildings where this method was used fell into ruin: the wood, however resistant, weakened with time, rotted and eventually disintegrated, leaving only an empty monolith. The latter, having lost its core, could no longer support the heavy weight of the upper masonry and broke, destroying the building.

The symbolism of the Khmer temple

One of the most original features of Khmer architecture is the sanctuary built on a tiered pyramid, which every major ruler probably felt he had to build as a sign of his power and which 19th-century archaeologists christened the temple-mountain.

Every Southeast Asian country that came under the influence of India found a different way of resolving the problem of how to reproduce the abode of the gods in the world of humans. As we have almost no idea of the rules governing the construction of

All the wooden buildings have disappeared. Only images on bas-reliefs (above) remain, showing that they were built on stilts and were light and very airy.

these sanctuaries, it is difficult to understand and explain their symbolism. Yet, in the light of some of the inscriptions, it is possible to establish a relationship between Mount Meru, the centre and axis of the universe in Indian cosmography, and certain temple-mountains in Angkor that are probably meant as the image, the representation on a human scale of Mount Meru.

The exceptionally wide terraces of the pyramid of Bakong (above) give this temple a special majesty. The main tower-sanctuary is from a later date.

From Bakong to Phnom Bakheng, an example of development

One of the most famous temple-mountains was built on the summit of Phnom Bakheng in the early 10th century, in the centre of the city of Yashodharapura. Sited on one of the few *phnoms* in the region, this monument was planned as a square pyramid with five storeys (centre and axis of the city) and can in fact be identified with Mount Meru. The temple reflects, in very complex fashion, the symbolic principles already found in the Bakong founded by Indravarman I in Hariharalaya in 881.

The broad development of Khmer architecture can be traced through a comparison of the two monuments. In Bakong, the summit of the five-storeyed artificial pyramid consists of a single tower-sanctuary, while in Phnom Bakheng the pyramid is crowned by five tower-sanctuaries in a quincunx. Twelve more small towers are situated on the fourth

Phnom Bakheng is set on a natural hill, which is why the pyramid-builders erected a series of twelve little sandstone temples on the terraces and crowned the hill with a quincunx of sandstone *prasats*, now in ruins (above).

terrace in Bakong, while twelve towers rise on each of the five terraces of the Phnom Bakheng pyramid.

Forty-four large brick tower-sanctuaries surround the base of the Phnom Bakheng pyramid, while only eight comparable towers are distributed around that of the Bakong pyramid. This architecture, unique in the Indianized world, culminated three centuries later in the masterpieces of Khmer architecture, the temples of Angkor Wat and the Bayon.

Phnom Bakheng, the chosen abode of the gods, is one of the few hills in the Angkor region, dominating the plain (in the background) and, beyond it, the western *baray*.

The monuments of the classical period of Angkor – Pre Rup, Banteay Srei, Baphuon and the great Angkor Wat, to mention only a few – are sufficient in themselves to establish the prestige of Khmer art. Beyond the capital, other lesser-known sites also contributed to its reputation. At its height, Khmer influence extended throughout continental Southeast Asia, from Myanmar (Burma) in the north to the China Sea in the south.

CHAPTER 4

THE CLASSICAL AGE OF ANGKOR

The vertical and horizontal lines of Angkor Wat contrast with the soft curves of the *nagas* flanking the raised causeway that leads to the pyramid (opposite). The same sense of balance can be seen in Angkor statuary, such as this dancing female divinity (right) from Koh Ker.

Under the reigns of Jayavarman IV and his successor (928–44), the capital was moved about 80 km (50 miles) north-east of Angkor to the site of Koh Ker. The reasons for this move, whether political, economic or religious, are hard to fathom. Before his accession to the throne, Jayavarman IV had already founded a very large temple in the city of Koh Ker, which he ruled; perhaps he did not want to leave it. Even if the court, accompanied by the protective divinity of the kingdom, as the inscriptions specify, did indeed leave Yashodharapura (that is Angkor), it is unlikely that this site was totally abandoned.

Angkor once again becomes the capital

The kings returned to Angkor under the reign of Rajendravarman (944–68), a great ruler – he is said to have won a military campaign against the Chams in about 950 – and an equally great builder, as he is responsible for the majestic temples of the East Mebon and Pre Rup. During his reign, the splendid foundations of several wealthy dignitaries reflected the importance attached to the administration. One such dignitary, the Brahman Yajnavaraha, guru of the future Jaravarman V, consecrated one of the most beautiful Angkor monuments in Cambodia, the temple of Banteay Srei, the 'citadel of women', in 967, the year before Rajendravarman's death.

The dense and elaborate decoration of this lintel from the East Mebon (953) shows Indra with a score of tiny figures (above). On the left and right, a curious and playful motif, an elephant astride its own trunk, which is transformed into the hindquarters of a horse.

The architecture and sculpture of Koh Ker are on a monumental scale: these hands, about 40 cm (16 inches) high, come from a statue of the five-headed and ten-armed Shiva, an exceptional work which looters probably broke very long ago in the hope of discovering treasure beneath the pedestal.

During the long reign of Jayavarman V (968–1000 or 1001), who came to the throne at a very early age, the authority of several dignitaries increased, probably to the detriment of the king's. The buildings that can probably be ascribed to his reign are: the enclosure of the Royal Palace, in which virtually every king lived henceforth; two buildings, North and South Khleang, constructed on an unusual (rectangular) ground plan and whose purpose is still not clear – the name means 'emporium' but monuments of this importance must have been religious; and, although not definitely, the Phimeanakas pyramid in the enclosure of the Royal Palace – the temple itself served as a private 'chapel' for the kings; and all or part of the large temple-mountain of Ta Keo, the least finished of the Angkor temples, a huge, five-tiered and almost unadorned pyramid.

The Shivaist temple of Banteay Srei (967) owes its modern name to its small size – the three *prasats* (below, the southern one) are less than 10 metres (c. 33 feet) high – and to the female figures decorating the walls of the north and south towers (opposite right). Like the young *dvarapalas* (or

guardians of the doors) of the central sanctuary (opposite left), these graceful *devatas* introduce a new suppleness into Khmer sculpture. Unusually, the temple decoration is complete and has been well preserved thanks to the quality of its pink sandstone. The pediments of the two libraries in the first enclosure contain magnificent narrative bas-reliefs in an undulating frame. The east pediment of the southern 'library' depicts Kailasa, Shiva's sacred mountain, being shaken by the demon Ravana (left, above and below).

The three main sanctuaries of Banteay Srei were built on a terrace reached via six little stairways. They were flanked by *ganas*, hybrid figures, lower divinities who were followers of the god

Shiva. These guardian figures are represented in the traditional manner: kneeling, with one hand holding an attribute that is presumably a weapon. Most are dressed in a *sampot*, a small garment draped round the hips, and some of them also wear splendid head-dresses (opposite, *gana* with the head of a monkey and *gana* with the head of a bird of prey). Their aggressive expressions reflect their role as guardians (left, a *gana* with a lion's head). The *gana* with a human head (above) has a fierce look, usually rendered in Khmer sculpture by protruding eyes, teeth and curled hair.

The Royal Palace

The Royal Palace of Angkor Thom extends over a rectangular area of 600 metres (about 1970 feet) east to west by 250 metres (820 feet) north to south. Its surrounding wall, made of laterite, has five *gopuras* or gateways: two to the north, two to the south and one to the east. Despite several excavations, not enough is yet known about the Royal Palace, which is still undergoing archaeological research. Many of the reconstructions within the enclosure can be attributed to Jayavarman VII, especially the pools in the northern part, with their terraces decorated with bas-reliefs. The palace buildings were all constructed of wood and have, of course, not survived.

Despite a century of excavations, it is still not known what the Royal Palace looked like originally because this enclosure has been altered so much. It is, however, certain that the two large complexes were clearly demarcated, with an official area in the east, no doubt meant for royal audiences, and a private area occupied by the apartments, the gynaeceum and the outbuildings. The plan shows: the reservoirs in

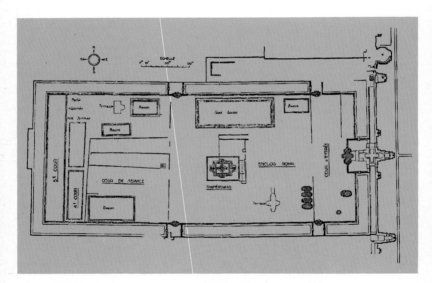

'We all offer our life and our grateful devotion to His Majesty Shri Suryavarmadeva'

Historically, the situation at the end of the 10th century and the beginning of the 11th was very confused. Following a dispute about the accession to the throne, Suryavarman I was crowned in 1010.

the north; in the centre, the Phimeanakas; on the right, preceded by a vast terrace, the eastern gateway marking the entrance; on the left, the courtyards, apartments and service areas.

The *gopuras* of the Royal Palace date from the reign of Jayavarman V. The royal terraces built at the time of Jayavarman VII (1181–1218?) have superseded the eastern *gopuras* (left). The pools in the northern part of the palace (centre) seem to have been intended for recreation.

It is not difficult to imagine the splendour of the royal feast days in this enchanting environment. The small temple-mountain of Phimeanakas (left) was a kind of 'chapel' within the palace enclosure, probably built in the 10th century on the site of an earlier temple.

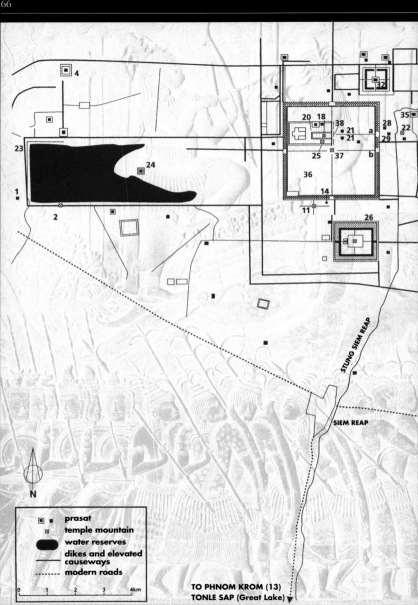

N

prasat
temple mountain
water reserves
dikes and elevated causeways
modern roads

0 1 2 3 4km

TO PHNOM KROM (13)
TONLE SAP (Great Lake) ▼

SIEM REAP

STUNG SIEM REAP

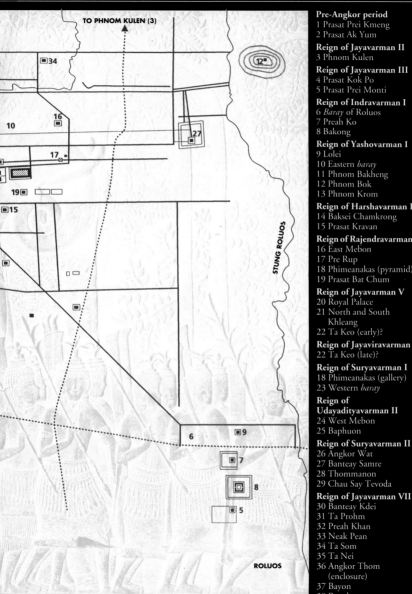

Pre-Angkor period
1 Prasat Prei Kmeng
2 Prasat Ak Yum

Reign of Jayavarman II
3 Phnom Kulen

Reign of Jayavarman III
4 Prasat Kok Po
5 Prasat Prei Monti

Reign of Indravarman I
6 *Baray* of Roluos
7 Preah Ko
8 Bakong

Reign of Yashovarman I
9 Lolei
10 Eastern *baray*
11 Phnom Bakheng
12 Phnom Bok
13 Phnom Krom

Reign of Harshavarman I
14 Baksei Chamkrong
15 Prasat Kravan

Reign of Rajendravarman I
16 East Mebon
17 Pre Rup
18 Phimeanakas (pyramid)?
19 Prasat Bat Chum

Reign of Jayavarman V
20 Royal Palace
21 North and South
   Khleang
22 Ta Keo (early)?

Reign of Jayaviravarman
22 Ta Keo (late)?

Reign of Suryavarman I
18 Phimeanakas (gallery)
23 Western *baray*

**Reign of
Udayadityavarman II**
24 West Mebon
25 Baphuon

Reign of Suryavarman II
26 Angkor Wat
27 Banteay Samre
28 Thommanon
29 Chau Say Tevoda

Reign of Jayavarman VII
30 Banteay Kdei
31 Ta Prohm
32 Preah Khan
33 Neak Pean
34 Ta Som
35 Ta Nei
36 Angkor Thom
   (enclosure)
37 Bayon
38 Royal terraces

This pediment from the temple of Preah Vihear (left) depicts one of the favourite subjects of Khmer art: the churning of the ocean of milk. The gods and demons churned the ocean of milk in order to obtain the liquid of immortality. As they did so, various treasures emerged, including Lakshmi, wife of Vishnu, Airavata, the three-headed elephant of Indra, and the *apsaras* or heavenly nymphs. Opposite right: aerial view of the Baphuon.

In 1011, in an attempt to confirm his nascent power, the king made his officials swear an oath of allegiance to him and had the text of this oath engraved on the eastern gate-pavilion of the Royal Palace enclosure. This period provides the best documentation on the difficulties that often accompanied changes of rule.

Although Suryavarman I was one of the greatest Khmer kings, he did not undertake any major architectural work in Angkor itself, unlike many of his predecessors and successors. He constructed the gallery of the third terrace of Phimeanakas, which is important as the first-known example of a stone-vaulted gallery, and probably began the construction of the western *baray*. Outside Angkor he was responsible, in part, for the construction of the remarkable temples of Phnom Chisor, Wat Ek and Wat Baset and for important foundations in Preah Vihear.

Udayadityavarman II and the Baphuon

Returning to the tradition of the builder-kings, Udayadityavarman II (1050–66) completed the

western *baray* – or perhaps built it from scratch if Suryavarman I is not believed to be the 'founding father' – while at the same time constructing the West Mebon, a small but highly interesting temple. Its central well may, it seems, have indicated the level of the *baray* waters. That is where the most spectacular and perhaps most beautiful Khmer bronze known to date was discovered in 1936, a colossal but, alas, fragmentary image of the god Vishnu in his aspect of Anantashayin.

In addition to these impressive works, Udayadityavarman II was also responsible for the Baphuon, noted for its narrative bas-reliefs that are both simple and touching; it is one of the most

The image of Vishnu Anantashayin – stretched out on the snake Ananta ('without end') – alludes to a myth of the creation of the world. When the four-armed god awakened, after a period between two cosmic eras, a lotus, on which Brahma soon appeared, emerged from his navel; the creator of the cosmos embarked on a new cycle of creation. The colossal bust from the West Mebon (left) – more than 2 metres (6½ feet) wide – is the largest antique bronze sculpture discovered so far in Cambodia.

daring temple-mountains, although it has suffered much destruction in the course of its history. At present it is the largest EFEO (Ecole française d'Extrême-Orient) site in Angkor, which architects and restorers are trying to reconstruct after the restoration work was interrupted in the early 1970s.

Times of war

There are inscriptions from the reign of Harshavarman III (1066–80?), the younger brother of Udayadityavarman II, that describe a campaign against Champa and the Cham response to this aggression in the form of a victorious raid against the Sambor region on the Mekong. From that period, relations between the Khmer people and the Chams became complex; sometimes allies, sometimes enemies, the two people henceforth shared a common destiny, often marked by conflict.

From 1080 to 1107 the throne was occupied by Jayavarman VI, a native of the city of Mahidharapura, a town that was probably situated in the north of the Khmer Empire. The inscriptions suggest that Jayavarman VI, the son of a local petty king, was not 'connected' to his predecessors on the throne of Angkor. It seems that there was a change of dynasty or even that he was a usurper.

At that time the royal family was in a sense dependent on two masters. One was the successor of Jayavarman VI, Dharanindravarman; the other, whose name is unknown, was certainly a 'legitimate' heir of Harshavarman III.

The young Suryavarman II (1113–45 or later), who was one of the greatest kings of Angkor, was related through his mother to the kings of Mahidharapura. Inscriptions show that he cannot have been more

These bas-reliefs, arranged in superimposed panels or horizontal bands on some of the pavilions of Baphuon, give an animated and naive picture of episodes from the Indian epics, such as the battle of Lanka in the *Ramayana* (below).

The balanced composition of this *gopura* from the temple of Banteay Samre (opposite) is typical of the architecture from the reign of Suryavarman II.

than twenty years old when he seized the throne and started his dazzling career. At least this seems likely from Cham inscriptions of the time that repeatedly tell of the king's military campaigns against Champa and its northern neighbour, Dai Viet, which had recently gained independence from China.

The splendour of Angkor Wat

Thommanon, Chau Say Tevoda, Banteay Samre, Beng Mealea and, in particular, Angkor Wat, reflect the glory of a reign without parallel in architecture.

Suryavarman II (above) is depicted twice in the west wing of the south gallery of bas-reliefs in Angkor Wat. Here he is shown enthroned in majesty talking with the Brahmans of the court (one of whom holds a manuscript in his hands, perhaps a list of the army dignitaries marching past the king in the lower level). Remarkable for their sophistication, the bas-reliefs of Angkor Wat are the work of artists who managed to render three dimensions in a technique reminiscent of chiselling. Following foldout pages: the churning of the ocean of milk, central part (eastern gallery, south wing); the battle of Lanka (western gallery, north wing); east–west section and plan of Angkor Wat.

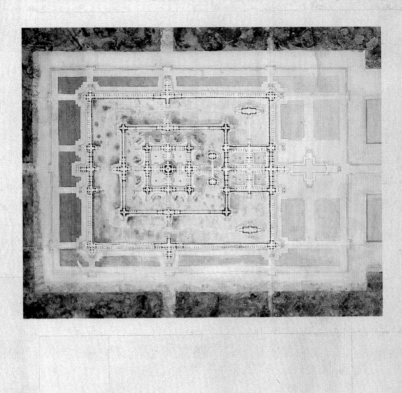

The great Vaishnavite temple of Angkor Wat – Suryavarman II was a worshipper of Vishnu – is without doubt the most beautiful of all the Khmer monuments and the most perfect in architectural and ornamental terms. Although it is not certain whether these sanctuaries were commissioned by the king himself, they all bear the hallmark of that period: balanced lines, sophisticated decoration in terms of both composition and technique. As in the past, dignitaries were responsible for work in many sites (including Preah Vihear, Wat Phu, Phnom Da and Hariharalaya). This period is regarded as a classical age, marked as always by the search for perfection but also, exceptionally, by its near achievement.

Angkor Wat, the state temple Suryavarman II built during the first half of the 12th century, is

The true size of Angkor Wat can only be appreciated from the air. The pyramid rises up in a landscape that is now empty but must at one time have contained many buildings. Conventional wisdom attributes its construction to Vishvakarman, the architect of the gods. And the temple is indeed unique in its design, use of perspective and decoration (right, two *apsaras*).

surrounded by a moat almost 250 metres (about 820 feet) wide. It occupies an area 1500 metres (approximately 4920 feet) east to west and 1300 metres (approximately 4260 feet) north to south. From the western entrances to the base of the actual pyramid, the faithful would follow a raised causeway bordered by *naga* balustrades. This pyramid, faced entirely in sandstone, is made up of three terraces supporting a quincunx of tower-sanctuaries whose roofs have very curious slightly convex contours. Each terrace is flanked by a vaulted gallery; the first-storey gallery and its two north-western and south-western pavilions contain the most beautiful narrative Khmer bas-reliefs, real masterpieces of world art. The epic or even historical subjects of these bas-reliefs – for instance the relief on the west wing of the southern gallery shows Suryavarman II's troops on parade – exalt the god Vishnu and, by association, the king himself. The monument was dedicated to Vishnu, which explains why, exceptionally, its entrance faces west and not east like nearly all the other temples. Light and lively cohorts of female divinities, *apsaras* and *devatas*, decorate the temple walls, clothed in sumptuous costumes and adorned with elaborate jewels.

The three terraces are crowned by a central tower reaching 60 metres (nearly 200 feet) above the ground.

Water, air, stone: three elements embodied by the temple. At Angkor Wat (above) the water of the reservoirs reflects the five towers of the quincunx; air, omnipresent, wafts gently through balustraded windows; stone, delicately incised with low-relief decoration, seems to shiver in time with the slow movements of the *apsaras*.

Left: general view of the pyramid from the northwest. Below: the gallery of bas-reliefs, with a play of light and shade. Opposite below: view down into the north side of the second-terrace gallery. Below left: splendid female divinities from Angkor Wat. Below: part of the third-storey axial stairway.

'A ll the creatures that are plunged in the ocean of existences, let me draw them from it by virtue of this good work. Let all the kings of Cambodia, devoted to the good, who will protect my foundation, attain with their line, their women, their dignitaries, their friends, the abode of deliverance where there is no more sickness.'

Stanzas XLVI–XLVII of the stele of the Hospitals

CHAPTER 5

THE TRIUMPH OF BUDDHISM

I n the art from the reign of Jayavarman VII, the faces verge on the sublime. This characteristic applies both to the imperious faces of the kings who guard the cardinal points, looking out into the world (left, at Angkor Thom) and to the lovely slender face of Queen Jayarajadevi, wife of Jayavarman VII, that expresses a sense of inner pathos (right).

The glory of the first half of the 12th century gave way to troubled times for the Khmer Empire. Yashovarman II succeeded Suryavarman II sometime after 1150 and ruled until 1165, the year he was probably assassinated and replaced on the throne by a usurper – as the inscriptions call him – by the name of Tribhuvanadityavarman. The latter headed the empire, during what appear to have been very difficult times, until 1177, one of the blackest years in Khmer history, marked by the seizure and sacking of the capital by the Cham armies of Jaya Indravarman IV.

Jayavarman VII, the Buddhist king

Shortly after what was no doubt a genuine national disaster, a prince, the future Jayavarman VII, set out to reconquer the country and, after driving out the Chams, was crowned king in 1181. According to bas-reliefs and inscriptions, the Khmer people won the day after a naval battle that was probably waged on the Great Lake. For Cambodia, his reign opened a new period of dazzling conquests (Jayavarman VII led his armies further afield than any of his predecessors), accompanied by intense creative activity (in architecture and statuary) that was closely linked to a remarkable change in religion: a complex form of Buddhism (Mahayana) was elevated to the state religion by this pious king, described

Jayavarman VII is the only Khmer king of whom portraits seem to exist. The monarch was depicted at various periods during his life. Below: the famous head from Preah Khan in Kompong Svay shows him in the prime of life. The face betrays some of the apparently contradictory aspects of his personality: will of iron and force of character on the one hand, profound Buddhist faith and peaceful meditation on the other.

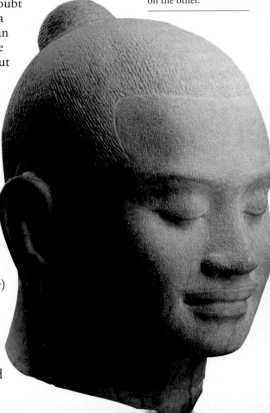

This triad (left) embodies the Buddhist precepts of the age of Jayavarman VII: wisdom and compassion. Prajnaparamita (left figure) is, among others, the 'incarnation' of one of the main Mahayana Buddhist texts; Lokeshvara (right figure) is the purest expression of love for all living beings; these two components are combined in the Buddha (central figure), who embodies the idea of Enlightenment. Below: Hevajra, the god with eight heads and sixteen arms, dances on the four Mara, symbols of the obstacles to spiritual progress.

on an inscription as being more moved by the suffering of his people than by his own.

His entire reign was indeed marked by this Buddhist compassion, expressed in one of the masterpieces of Khmer art, the famous 'smile of Angkor'. Although the archetypal image of the Khmer Buddha, the Buddha protected by the *naga* Mucilinda, first appeared in statuary during the final years of the 10th century when the iconography of what is known as Tantric Buddhism was becoming established, it was not until the reign of Jayavarman VII that Buddhist art reached its aesthetic high point, with a definite return towards realism.

Jayavarman VII had a considerable number of monuments constructed – in fact it is said that he built more than all his predecessors taken together. Many temples are attributed to his reign, both in Angkor and in the provinces. They include Ta Prohm (1186), dedicated to his mother and to his guru, Preah Khan (1191), dedicated to his father, Banteay

Archaeologists have deliberately left the temple of Ta Prohm in its 'natural state' in order to preserve the special ambience of Angkor as it was seen by the first western explorers to 'discover' it in the 19th century. The appeal of this site derives as much from the chaotic aspect of the ruins as from the oppressive vegetation smothering the buildings. However, the site suffers from some basic defects. It was constructed with a lack of care and developed in stages, giving rise to a complex ground plan and small areas that are crowded with additional passages, galleries and sanctuaries.

Kdei, Ta Som, Neak Pean, the royal terraces – the Elephant Terrace, from which the king and his court watched processions and important celebrations, and the Leper King Terrace, which may well have been used for cremations (as suggested by the statue of Yama, judge of the dead, that used to stand there) – but also Banteay Chmar, to mention only one major provincial temple complex, which was in fact a proper city.

A bove: aerial view of the heart of the Preah Khan ('sacred sword') complex, which, together with Ta Prohm, is one of the largest-scale temples on the Angkor site. A great many people lived here (priests of the sanctuary, servants, dancers). Situated on the central islet of the *baray* of Preah Khan, the small temple of Neak Pean (left) is a unique and original monument. It is made up of a single tower surrounded by quadrilateral pools. The circular base of the *prasat* itself is surrounded by two *nagas* with intertwined tails.

He provided his empire with an extensive network of communication lines, equipped with numerous (121) 'stop-overs'. However, even though he accomplished much in this area, Cambodia was no doubt not entirely lacking in infrastructure at the time. There are inscriptions that explicitly attribute to him the construction of 102 hospitals, indicating his concern for the welfare of his people. It is also clear how they were run, thanks to details given in some of the foundation steles.

Angkor Thom and the Bayon: the town and its temple

Yet the masterpiece of his reign remains the town of Angkor Thom with its 12

The temple of the Bayon was intended by Jayavarman VII as a pantheon of all the divinities of the empire. The many inscriptions at the entry to the chapels and tower-sanctuaries list the gods who used to live there. The complexity of this monument (in terms of its plan – exceptionally, the central tower is circular – iconography and symbolism) is such that various interpretations have been suggested by scholars. The alterations made in the course of its construction make it even more difficult to understand.

kilometres (over 7 miles) of walls and the temple in the centre, the Bayon. Some of the bas-reliefs in the external gallery of the Bayon depict everyday life, or at least some aspects of it, in late 12th- and early 13th-century Cambodia. It was at this time that Angkor reached the height of its power and glory and these scenes provide a lively and touching picture of a civilization of which only the more official, rather cold and distant side had been seen in the past.

In fact these bas-reliefs only make up a part of the extremely rich iconography of the monument, which virtually assembled all the divinities of the empire, whether Buddhist, Brahmanist or other, under the aegis of the Buddha.

The town as image

The most constant feature of Khmer architecture is that it is 'architecture as image'. The inscriptions on certain monuments often contain references to Indian cosmography. The 'representation' of Mount Meru is certainly the most familiar example, although there are others, such as Angkor Thom and the Bayon, that can be interpreted in several ways. The Bayon-Mount Mandara equivalence, symbolized by the giants clasping the body of an

There are some surprising features in the Bayon. Two concentric surrounding galleries are decorated with bas-reliefs depicting historical and Brahmanist subjects that would not usually be found in a Buddhist temple. It is also difficult to identify the faces on the towers of the second and third terraces, which certainly bear no relation to the Buddha or Jayavarman VII himself. The only possible hypothesis, taking a global approach to the architectural symbolism, is that the three main temples – the Bayon, Preah Khan and Ta Prohm (dedicated to the Buddha, Lokeshvara and Prajnaparamita) – erected by Jayavarman VII were intended as a triad.

In the Bayon, the well-known bas-reliefs on the lower panel of the outer gallery depict scenes from everyday life. They are valuable sources of information on aspects of Angkor civilization at the beginning of the 13th century. Opposite above: a family accompanies a military detachment (note the cart that is identical to those still seen today in the Cambodian countryside). Left: a stall selling fish. Below: cooks working in a tent (from left to right: servants carrying in the food, cooking a pig and other dishes, preparing brochettes).

enormous snake (the churning-rope) which causes the mountain (the churning-stick) to pivot and churn the ocean, as the *devas* (gods) and *asuras* (anti-gods or, by extension, demons) used to do in times immemorial, has long been put forward (by Paul Mus) as an explanation of the plan of the city. In Hindu mythology, the purpose of churning the ocean was to

Above: the face towers of the Bayon, omnipresent and ubiquitous. Below: the 'giants' causeway', 100 metres (c. 328 feet) long, leading up to the southern gate of Angkor Thom.

obtain the liquid of immortality, *amrita*. The myth of
the churning of the ocean of milk also explains why
Angkor Thom, the city of Jayavarman VII, was
regarded as a fount of treasures, of blessings, of
wealth, and over and above that as the very source of
the empire's prosperity. At the same time the *naga* or
sacred snake is also the symbol of the rainbow, the
bridge linking the secular to the divine world.

However, another interpretation can also be put
forward to explain the symbolism of Angkor Thom.
The Bayon, with its countless towers with faces, could
be a magnificent allusion to the Assembly Hall of
the Gods, Sudhammasabha, in Buddhist cosmology
(Jean Boisselier). In that sense the remarkable faces
on the temple could be a reference to the Brahma
Sanankumara ('ever young') who pass on the
Buddha's teachings not only to all the Buddhist
but also to the Hindu divinities who meet from
time to time in that hall. Angkor Thom thus
appears to be the earthly replica of the city of
Indra, king of the gods, of which this shrine
forms the centre. Situated on the summit of
Mount Meru, the city of Indra is also
guarded by the Four Great Kings, guardians

The two rows of fifty-four giants (*devas* and *asuras*) supporting the body of a gigantic *naga* in front of the five gateways of the city can be regarded as its defenders.

of the cardinal points, and it is probably their faces that can be seen on the monumental gates of Angkor Thom.

The various interpretations that have been put forward to explain the significance of Angkor Thom are of course not mutually exclusive and it is indeed probable that they overlap. Finally, it is worth noting that the actual plan of the Bayon reflects the structure of a *mandala*; originally it contained in its centre an image of the Buddha protected by the *naga*. The statue of this Buddha was found during excavations carried out in 1933 in the central sanctuary that was formally reconsecrated in 1935. It is now housed in a pavilion not far from the temple.

Towards another world

Although Jayavarman VII is now regarded as the greatest of all the Cambodian kings thanks to his achievements, his frenzy to conquer and construct must have seemed a heavy burden for his people at

The Bayon, almost shapeless seen from ground level, becomes more legible viewed from the air, from where only the gods could see it. The overall ground plan (circular central sanctuary and concentric square enclosures) is that of a *mandala*, a complex diagram representing the 'world' of a divinity. The Bayon temple is devoted to Buddhism.

the time. It is sometimes said that his reign, during which Khmer influence and the extent of the empire grew to previously unknown heights, left his people drained of energy; and it is true that not one great monument was built in Angkor after Jayavarman VII.

The bas-reliefs of the Bayon contain scenes of war in which the Chams, recognizable by their tiered head-dresses, are likened to *asuras*. They are fighting

Indeed, orthodox Brahmans, who obviously did not appreciate the religious changes imposed by the king, reacted strongly under the reign of his second successor, Jayavarman VIII (1243–95). Numerous images of the Buddha on the monuments of Jayavarman VII were destroyed.

the Khmer, who wear a little chignon on their heads. The latter are equal to *devas*, in a metaphor suggesting the Khmer were superior to the Chams.

The post-Angkor period

Until the mid-14th century there was still much the same political and religious continuity in Angkor as in the past. Gradually, however, Khmer civilization underwent one of the most profound and enduring changes it had ever seen since the spread of Indian religions during the first centuries AD: the adoption, on a vast and indeed national scale, of Theravada Buddhism (the original Buddhism, literally the 'path or doctrine of the elders'), which remains the religion of Cambodia today.

This phase of cultural transition was accompanied, although the two events were not linked, by the political weakening of the empire together with the emergence of new powers in continental Southeast Asia. Cambodia was now exposed to the expansionist ambitions of its neighbours, in particular the Thais from the kingdom of Ayuthaya, and the capital

This Buddha (above), from the second half of the 13th century or 14th century, still reflects the grandeur and expressiveness of the art of the Bayon but portrays it in a more relaxed and human manner, in the spirit of Theravada Buddhism. Left: the lacquered wood worshipper from Angkor Wat (15th?– 16th century) is one of the most remarkable post-Angkor works. The influence of the Siamese art of Ayuthaya is perceptible here (in the clothing and headdress), while the reserved and almost severe expression is still typically Khmer.

came under attack on several occasions. Tired of war after the repeated attacks from Siam, the monarchy abandoned Angkor in 1431, the year most frequently given for the beginning of the post-Angkor period, though it would perhaps be more logical to date it to the 14th century, to the time when Theravada Buddhism was adopted definitively. In this way it would be possible to take more account of developments in the arts, especially architecture,

which turned resolutely towards the use of wood from that period, and of changes in language, for it was in the 14th century that Sanskrit gave way to Pali in the inscriptions. However, history does not lend itself to rigid divisions and in Cambodia the demarcation of historical periods seems to fluctuate depending on the viewpoint adopted.

The post-Angkor period saw the adoption of Theravada Buddhism. This profound religious change was reflected in art by the transition to statuary entirely different in spirit from Angkor sculpture: grandeur and show gave way to humility and restraint. Similarly, a new kind of architecture gained ground: the transition from building in stone to building in wood, new types of buildings such as the *chedi* (a Southeast Asian adaptation of the Indian *stupa*) and the *vihar* (a rectangular sanctuary covered by a double-sloped roof and often surrounded by a peristyle). Sadly, this fragile heritage has almost entirely disappeared, a victim of war and perishable building materials. In a very few cases, Angkor sanctuaries were modified. Three of the pediments of the sanctuary of Wat Nokor (13th century) were resculpted in about 1566. The one on the west (left) shows a scene from the life of the Buddha: Prince Siddhartha before leaving his palace to embark on the spiritual journey that was to lead him to Enlightenment.

Although sources disagree about the date (some documents give 1369, others 1432), it is traditionally accepted that the court settled in Srei Santhor under the reign of Ponhea Yat. Yet the court did not remain in the new capital for very long, as it appears that the region suffered from frequent and severe flooding. Ponhea Yat therefore chose a new site, Chadomukh, the future Phnom Penh, although Srei Santhor still remained the royal residence and was occupied on

Above: the hill of Udong on which the funerary *chedis* of certain 19th- and early 20th-century monarchs were erected (see p. 96). Below: the gigantic reclining Buddha (16th century) on the western side of the Baphuon.

several occasions until the end of the 17th century. The king and his court also settled at other sites – such as Lovek and Udong – for varying periods.

During the second half of the 16th century, under the reign of Ang Chan I (1516–66) or his son, Paramaraja I (1566–76), Angkor was once again, and for the last time, occupied by the Khmer kings. This period saw the completion of some of the bas-reliefs of Angkor Wat (in the north-east quadrant of the gallery of bas-reliefs) and possibly, though not definitely, the construction of a number of large-scale works, such as the colossal images of the Buddha in the Baphuon and on the summit of Phnom Bakheng.

It is easy to view the whole of Khmer civilization with reference to the splendid site of Angkor alone, although it cannot embody all the richness, diversity and grandeur of Khmer art. However, it was this site that fascinated western travellers who discovered the mysterious capital, smothered in vegetation, during the 19th century. Since then Cambodia has slowly begun to reveal the marvels of its past.

The smiling face of this stone bust of an adorned Buddha (15th–16th century) looks severe. However, many other Post-Angkor works of art illustrate the gentleness characteristic of the era.

DOCUMENTS

The spread of Indian culture in Southeast Asia

Any attempt to understand the culture of Southeast Asia, and Cambodia in particular, must take account of Indian influence. According to George Coedès, scholar of epigraphical studies and author of the first modern work on the subject, this Indianization developed in its own individual way in Southeast Asia to produce highly original works of art.

The history of the expansion of Indian civilization to the east has not yet been told in its entirety. We are beginning to be familiar with the results of this expansion in the various countries considered separately, but we are reduced to hypotheses concerning its origins and its processes. I do not pretend to solve these problems.... I shall only attempt to assemble the results that have been established and to set down some general traits common to all the Indianized kingdoms of Farther India.

I have so far, for the sake of convenience, used the terms 'Indianization' and 'expansion of Indian culture' as if they referred to a simple historical fact that took place in a specific epoch. This concept must be made more precise.... The relations between India proper and Farther India date back to prehistoric times. But from a certain period on, these relations resulted in the founding of Indian kingdoms on the Indochinese Peninsula and in the islands of Indonesia. The oldest archaeological remains these states have left us are not necessarily evidence of the first civilizing wave. It is probable, *a priori*, that the priests who consecrated the first Brahmanic or Buddhist sanctuaries and the scholars who composed the first Sanskrit inscriptions were preceded by seamen, traders, or immigrants – founders of the

The Buddha in the Indian style (7th century).

first Indian settlements. These settlements, in turn, were not always entirely new creations; in many cases (Oc Eo in Cochin China, Kuala Selinsing in Perak, Sempaga in the Celebes, etc.), they were built on Neolithic sites that the seamen from India had frequented perhaps from time immemorial.

The coming of the Indians to Southeast Asia cannot be compared to the arrival of the Europeans in America, for in this part of the world the newcomers were not strangers discovering new lands. At some time that we must try to date, following circumstances that we can attempt to determine, the sporadic influx of traders and immigrants became a steady flow that resulted in the founding of Indian kingdoms practising the arts, customs and religions of India, and using Sanskrit as their sacred language....

The Indians were not confronted by uncultured 'savages' but, on the contrary, by people endowed with a civilization that had traits in common with the civilization of pre-Aryan India. The speed and ease with which the Aryanized Indians propagated their culture is undoubtedly explained in part by the fact that, in the customs and beliefs of these immigrants, the natives discovered, under an Indian veneer, a base common to all of monsoon India.

It is then neither a question of a contact between strangers or of a first contact. If the Indianization of Farther India around the beginning of the Christian Era seems to be a new development, it is because the Indians – who were not on their first voyage, but were arriving in greater numbers – were accompanied for the first time by educated elements capable of spreading the religions and arts of India and the Sanskrit language. The Indianization of Farther India is the continuation overseas of a 'Brahmanization' that had its earliest focus in Northwest India and that 'having begun well before the Buddha, continues to our day in Bengal as well as in the south'. And, in fact, the most ancient Sanskrit inscriptions of Farther India are not much later than the first Sanskrit inscriptions of India itself.

Indianization must be understood essentially as the expansion of an organized culture that was founded upon the Indian conception of royalty, was characterized by Hinduist or Buddhist cults, the mythology of the *Puranas*, and the observance of the *Dharmasastras*, and expressed itself in the Sanskrit language. It is for this reason that we sometimes speak of 'Sanskritization' instead of 'Indianization'.

This Sanskrit or Indian civilization, transplanted into Southeast Asia and called, according to the country, 'Indo-Khmer', 'Indo-Javanese', etc., is the one we are able to recognize in the epigraphical or archaeological documents.... [It] was the civilization of an elite and not that of the whole population, whose beliefs and way of life are still very insufficiently known. Since nothing more is known, it would be vain to try to arbitrate the conflict between those who hold that the indigenous societies have preserved the essence of their original character under an Indian veneer and those who believe they were integrated into a society of the Indian type.

George Coedès
The Indianized States of Southeast Asia,
translated by S. B. Cowing, 1971

Inscriptions, the basis of our knowledge of history

Since the first publication on the subject by the Dutch scholar Hendrik Kern in the late 19th century, Cambodian inscriptions, in Sanskrit and Khmer, have helped to uncover a lost past. The official section of these inscriptions relates not only to the gods to whom it is addressed but also to the kings who founded the monuments of ancient Cambodia (genealogies, panegyrics and eulogies). The other register, always written in Khmer, gives an account of the practicalities of relig- ious foundations, such as gifts of land and subsidies. The following inscriptions were originally translated by George Coèdes.

Stele at Tuol Neak Ta Bak Ka (K. 940)

This stele was found in January 1948, at a depth of 20 cm (8 inches), in a rice field in the khum *of Dangkor,* srok *of Phnom Penh, in the province of Kandal. It was reported to the Cambodian Criminal Investigation Department on 27 January because of the crowds of visitors who came to make offerings to this stone.…*

It is a rectangular stone, 90 cm high by 40 cm wide (about 35 by 16 inches), at the top of which is a sculpted bas-relief of a bull lying on a lotus throne (see picture on page 43). Below it, separated from the bas-relief by a band of pearl decoration, is a carved Khmer inscription of eleven lines in pre-Angkor characters with large downstrokes.

*This text is an order (*ajna*) given by a V. K. A. (meaning* Vrah Kamratem an, *or 'our Lord' in Khmer), perhaps an un- named king, for the delivery to the place known as Tirthagrama ('village of the wharf') of certain quantities of salt to the boats of several sanctuaries. An impreca- tion commonly used at the time concludes this text, which is interesting in that it shows that the region of Phnom Penh must have been a staging post on the salt road.*

This is the order of V. K. A: deliver to the boat of V. K. A. Shri Pingaleshvara 3 *knan* of salt; deliver to the boat of Kpon K. A. Kamratan Slot 3 *knan* of salt; deliver to the two boats of Sharvashrama 4 *knan* of salt; deliver to the boat of V. K. A. Shri Badreshvara 2 *knan* of salt; deliver to the boat of V. K. A. Shri Puskareshvara 2 *knan* of salt. This is to be distributed to Tirthagrama ('village of the wharf') by order of V. K. A.

Anyone who levies a tax on this, whether on arrival or departure, anyone who prevents this, anyone who infringes this order shall be punished.

Inscription at Baksei Chamkrong (K. 286)

One of the most remarkable Cambodian Sanskrit inscriptions is the one carved on the piers of the tower at Baksei Chamkrong. It is important because it is the only one to give a summary of the history of Cambodia from its beginnings up to the reign of Rajendravarman.

I. To Him who, although unique, in the heart of several … in his shining body, like the full moon at night … (homage to Parameshvara!) [Shiva]….

V. May the image of Parameshvara-Sharngin (Harihara), through which, by their contiguity, the brilliance inherent in each of them can be distinguished, procure success, as the Ganga does when it joins with the Yamuna, taking its part (of their common spouse) from its rival Ambika to whom it was (formerly) wedded.

VI. I worship the two Bhavas (Shiva and Uma), the spring of the universe, united in a single body, but divided into many conditions such as the *avyakta* and the *buddhi*, leading like the two paths of the Dharma (respectively) to heaven and to deliverance, pleasing to the heart, sparkling like the golden mountain and the snow mountain united….

IX. Victorious is the Ganga, whose mass of pure and sparkling drops falls from the sky where the crescent moon projects its horns and, in breaking the furling waves, produces an outburst of stars, like a broken necklace of precious stones.

X. May Lakshmi draw out the evil from your spirits, as she does from within the body of her husband of many forms. She whose unique beauty fills the entire universe – what need is there to speak of her other qualities?

XI. Honour Kambu Svayambhuva whose glory (like a star) has risen on the horizon, and whose good lineage, after uniting the solar race with the lunar race, removes all the *shastra* of ignorance [or: darkness], spreads his power [or: brightness], levies light taxes [or: gentle rays] and is accomplished in all the arts [or: has all the *kalas*].

XII. I implore Mera, the most illustrious of celestial women, whom Hara, guru of the three worlds, much desiring to outshine those begotten by Daksa thanks to his three eyes, has given from on high to the maharishi as his queen….

XVI. There then appeared the kings, of whom the first was Shri Rudravarman, deriving their origin from Shri Kaundinya and the daughter of Soma, spreading the brilliance of their glory in the three worlds, ably governing their subjects, possessing the *Shruti*….

XIX. From this lineage was born the fortunate and most glorious Jayavarman [II], who established his residence on the summit of Mahendra, who conquered the god of the hundred sacrifices (Indra) by a *kotihoma* and whose stool had become the touchstone of the royal diadems.

XX. Holding the land of Shri Kambu [or: the land, the conch and Shri], protector and adornment of the solar race [or: guardian of the playful cows of noble race], increasing the prosperity of the land [or: raising Mount Govardhana], destroyer of the underworld [or: (the *asura*) Naraka], victorious, vanquisher of flatterers [or: the snake], enemy of the law-breakers [or: enemy of Kamsa (or Vrsabha)], pearl of beauty … he had the brilliance of the lotus-eyed god (Vishnu)….

XXII. His victorious son, possessing an unvanquished fortune [or: the fortune of Vishnu], conqueror of his enemies, named Shri Jayavarman [III], was, perhaps as a result of his affection for the old, passionate about the science of antiquity and (although) young, without passion for the young Shri woman.

XXIII. A great politician, an able teacher, he led to merit and fortune his subjects who had no merit and fortune, by modifying them skilfully, like the man who knows the stages and wishes to achieve purity [or: endowed with method, a skilful master, he applied the *guna* and the *vrddhi* to a primitive form that was without *guna* and *vrddhi*, by modifying it precisely, like a man who knows the different stages, wishing to use (the root) *mrj* ('to purify')].

XXIV. His maternal uncle, resembling Indra, had the good fortune to beget a son named Shri Indravarman who, although established on earth with the title of Indra of men, enjoyed for a long time the (celestial) pleasures of the abode of Indra.

XXV. When he mounted his throne covered in the webbing (formed by) the rays of their jewels, the diadems of the kings fell from their heads to his feet, as the stars (fall) from the sky at sunrise.

XXVI. On the earth he placed a *linga* of the husband of Uma going by the name of Shri Indreshvara with the images of Shridhara, Ambika and others, and he dug a pool; at the cardinal points (he placed) his brilliant glory and (he undermined) the force of his enemies.

XXVII. His son without equal, bedecked in glory, was given the name Shri Yashovarman [I] and was the supreme master of the land that is bordered by the Suksma-Kamrata, the ocean, China and the Champa.

XXVIII. 'He who is seated on the lotus (Brahma) is ever desirous of adorning (with his presence) the

beautiful lotus of the navel of He who has a lotus in his navel (Vishnu)', it is without doubt in this spirit that Shambhu sat for so long on the lotus that is the heart of this man without equal [or: of this Vishnu].

XXIX. On the five summits of a Meru, as though on the five summits of the mountain (Mount Meru), and as though in an island of the great ocean, he set up more than one hundred gods, and he dug the pool of Yashodhara.

XXX. He had a well-beloved son, Shri Harshavarman [I], who was the joy of the universe and whose feet shone with the splendour of the garlands of rubies covering the diadems of the kings of the four cardinal points.

XXXI. A skilful swordsman, shining with glory, strict in meditation, hastening to the service of others, serious in his heroism, closed against evil, although endowed with the quality of goodness, he possessed the (other) two qualities in excess.

XXXII. In order to increase the Dharma of his parents, he obeyed the rule and erected here these images in gold of the two Ishvara (Shiva and Uma) and, at the foot of the Indradri, the images of the enemy of Mura (Vishnu) and of two *Devis*.

XXXIII. Then his younger son born of the same mother, Shri Ishanavarman [II], victorious, of a beauty surpassing love, dispelling the darkness, possessing all the arts [or: all the *kalas*], was a moon among kings....

XXXV. The husband of the sister of his father, the very able Shri Jayavarman [IV], inspired by Shri, founded a town which, by its size, became the seat of power of the Shris of the three worlds....

XXXVII. In Lingapura, in a high place, he erected – a difficult feat! – a *linga* of Sharva, placed at a height of nine times nine cubits, with the images of Brahma and other gods.

XXXVIII. His son Shri Harshavarman [II], the joy of all creatures, a conqueror burning with heroism, possessing a glory without equal, wise, had the power to make his commands inviolable....

XL. His brother, his elder in age and virtue, was King Shri Rajendravarman, who outshone the other kings by his royal powers and whose nascent virtues were sung by the world....

XLII. His charming beauty, the joy of a thousand eyes without exception from his birth, outshone the beauty of Love, which in the end provoked the anger of the three-eyed god (Shiva).

XLIII. Watered by the torrent of his donations [or: by the frontal liquid], including elephants and all manner of riches [or: produced by a multitude of elephants], and refreshed by many lotuses [or: many elephant trunks], the liana of his glory embraces all the rows of trees in the universe.

XLIV. In the town of Shiva he installed Siddheshvara, a miraculous *linga* of the Everlasting, glowing with a miraculous power, and in the island of the pool of Yashodhara, a *linga* and images.

XLV. This able king, endowed with a divine vision, added that incomparable golden image of Parameshvara, with the appropriate rites, and the splendour of this *prasat* decorated with stucco.

XLVI. Jupiter joined with Saturn is in Leo; Mars in Capricorn; Mercury with Venus in Aquarius; the sun rules in Pisces and the moon in Pusya; risen with Taurus, Shaka plays with the (eight) bodies, the (six) flavours and the number nine; being propitious, the planets, his *Gana*, act as *hotar* in the

Inscribed stele with Shiva and Parvati dating from 1069.

presence of the glorious Lord well-established in his abode.

XLVII. 'The just man supports the Dharma, the unjust destroys it, but of the two the first is the stronger'; in that spirit He whose mind has no limits (Rajendravarman) deems it futile to appeal to the goodwill of his successors (to maintain his foundation).

XLVIII. If that which belongs to the gods is destroyed through poor observance of the Dharma, the good man is innocent, in accordance with the repeated proclamations of the kings.

Om! Homage to Shiva!

The customs of Cambodia

Apart from inscriptions, the only record of the golden age of Angkor comes from the Chinese envoy Zhou Daguan, who visited the city from 1296 to 1297.

B ecause of the marks made by the lichens covering it, this statue of the god Yama (judge of the dead) was thought to represent a king suffering from leprosy, the famous 'Leper King'.

Cambodian dwellings

The Royal Palace, as well as official buildings and homes of the nobles, all face the east. The Royal Palace stands to the north of the Golden Tower and the Bridge of Gold; starting from the gate its circumference is nearly one and a half miles. The tiles of the central dwelling are of lead; other parts of the palace are covered with pottery tiles, yellow in colour. Lintels and columns, all decorated with carved or painted Buddhas, are immense. The roofs, too, are impressive. Long colonnades and open corridors stretch away, interlaced in harmonious relation. In the chamber where the sovereign attends to affairs of state, there is a golden window, with mirrors disposed on square columns to the right and left of the window-trim, forty or so in number. Below the window is a frieze of elephants. I have heard it said that within the palace are many marvellous sights, but these are so strictly guarded that I had no chance to see them.

Out of the palace rises a golden tower, to the top of which the ruler ascends nightly to sleep. It is common belief that in the tower dwells a genie, formed like a serpent with nine heads, which is Lord of the entire kingdom. Every night this genie appears in the shape of a woman, with whom the sovereign couples. Not even the wives of the King may enter here. At the second watch the King comes forth and is then free to sleep with his wives and his concubines. Should the genie fail to appear for a single night, it is a sign that the King's death is at hand. If, on the other hand, the King should fail to keep his tryst, disaster is sure to follow.

The dwellings of the princes and holders of high office are wholly different in size and design from those of the people. The family temple and the main hall are covered with tiles; all the outlying buildings are thatched with straw. The rank of every official determines the size of his house.

Straw thatch covers the dwellings of the commoners, not one of whom would dare place the smallest bit of tile on his roof. In this class, too, wealth determines the size of the house, but no one would venture to vie with the nobility.

Clothing

Every man or woman, from the sovereign down, knots the hair and leaves the shoulders bare. Round the waist they wear a small strip of cloth, over which a larger piece is drawn when they leave their houses. Many rules, based on rank, govern the choice of materials. Among the fabrics worn by the sovereign, are some, very rich and sheer, which are valued at three or four ounces of gold. Although certain fabrics are woven in Cambodia, many are imported from Siam and Champa, preference being given to the Indian weaving for its skill and delicacy.

Only the ruler may wear fabrics woven in an all-over pattern. On his head he carries a diadem much like those worn by the *vajradhara*; at times he lays aside the diadem and weaves into his hair a garland of fragrant blossoms reminding one of jasmine. Round his neck he wears some three pounds of great pearls. On wrists, ankles, and fingers he wears bracelets and rings of gold, all set with cat's-eyes. His feet are bare. The soles of his feet and the palms of his hands are stained red with henna. On leaving the palace he wears a golden sword.

Only the womenfolk of the commoners are permitted to stain the soles of their feet and the palms of their hands. This is forbidden to men. The wearing of fabrics patterned with recurring groups of flowers is permitted to high officers and princes. Ordinary mandarins are allowed to wear only material with two groups of flowers, and women of the people may do likewise. Should a Chinese, newly arrived, wear cloth with two groups of flowers, it cannot be charged against him, for he is *an-ting pa-sha* (*min-ting bhasa*), 'a man who does not know the rules'.

Functionaries

In this country there is a hierarchy of ministers, generals, astronomers and other functionaries; beneath these come all sorts of small employees, differing only in name from our own. For the most part princes are selected as office-holders; if not of princely rank they offer their daughters as royal concubines.

When functionaries go out in public, their insignia and the number of their attendants are regulated according to rank. The highest dignitaries use palanquins with golden shafts and four parasols with handles of gold; those next in rank have a palanquin with golden shafts and two gold-handled parasols; then come those entitled to one palanquin with gold shafts and one gold-handled parasol; and finally those with only a gold-handled parasol. Further down the line come those permitted only a silver-handled parasol, and there are others who use a palanquin with silver shafts. Functionaries entitled to gold parasols are called *pa-ting* (*mrateng*?) or *an-ting* (*am teng*); those with silver parasols are called *ssu-la-ti* (*sresthin*?). All parasols are made of red Chinese taffeta, with flounces falling to the ground. Water-proof parasols are all made of oiled green taffeta, and the flounces are short.

The natives

The customs common to all the southern barbarians are found throughout Cambodia, whose inhabitants are coarse people, ugly and deeply sunburned. This is true not only of those living in the remote fastnesses of the sea islands but of the dwellers in centres of population. It applies equally to the ladies of the court and to the womenfolk of the noble

heard it said that there are from three to five thousand of these, separated into various categories. They are seldom seen beyond the palace gates.

Every time I was admitted to the palace for an audience with the King, he came forward with his chief wife and took his seat in the embrasure of the golden window in the main audience hall. The ladies of the court were drawn up on both sides of the veranda below the window, changing places now and then to get a better look at us, and thus giving me a good chance to see them.

The Royal Palace of Angkor Thom seen from the Elephant Terrace.

houses, whose pallor, like that of jade, comes from being shuttered away from the fierce sunlight.

Generally speaking, the women, like the men, wear only a strip of cloth, bound round the waist, showing bare breasts of milky whiteness. Their hair is fastened up in a knot, and they go barefoot, even the wives of the King, who are five in number, one of whom dwells in the central palace and one at each of the four cardinal points. As for the concubines and palace girls, I have

When a beautiful girl is born into a family, no time is lost in sending her to the palace.

In a lower category are the women who do errands for the palace; of these, called *ch'en-chia-lan* (= Sanskrit *srnghara*) there are at least two thousand, all married, with homes throughout the city. The hair of the forehead is shaved high after the manner of the northern people and a vermilion mark is made here, as well as on each temple. This is the distinctive sign of the *ch'en-chia-lan*.

Only these women are given entry to the palace, which is forbidden to all of lesser rank. They move in an unbroken stream through the streets in front of and behind the palace.

Women of the people knot their hair, but there is no sign of hairpins or comb, or any other adornment of the head. On their arms they wear gold bracelets and rings of gold on their fingers: the palace women and the court ladies also observe this fashion. Men and women alike are anointed with perfumes compounded of sandalwood, musk, and other essences.

Worship of the Buddha is universal.

In the market place groups of ten or more catamites are to be seen every day, making efforts to catch the attention of the Chinese in the hope of rich presents. A revolting, unworthy custom, this!…

Slaves

Wild men from the hills can be bought to serve as slaves. Families of wealth may own more than one hundred; those of lesser means content themselves with ten or twenty; only the very poor have none. These savages are captured in the wild mountainous regions, and are of a wholly separate race called *Chuang* (brigands). After being brought to town, they dare not venture out of their owners' houses. So looked down on are these wretches that when, in the course of a dispute, a Cambodian is called 'Chuang' by his adversary, dark hatred strikes to the marrow of his bones.

If young and strong, slaves may be worth a hundred pieces of cloth; when old and feeble, they can be had for thirty or forty pieces. They are permitted to lie down or be seated only beneath the floor of the house. To perform their tasks they may go upstairs, but only after they have knelt, bowed to the ground, and joined their hands in reverence. Their master they call *pa-t'o* (*patau*, father); the mistress is addressed as *mi* (*me*, mother).

Cambodian justice

…Points of dispute between citizens, however trifling, are taken to the ruler. Unheard of is punishment administered by light or heavy bastinado, and penalties are, so I am told, only of a pecuniary nature. In dealing with cases of great seriousness, recourse is not had to strangulation or beheading; outside the West Gate, however, a ditch is dug into which the criminal is placed, earth and stones are thrown back and heaped high, and all is over.

Lesser crimes are dealt with by cutting off feet or hands, or by amputation of the nose. However, no punishment is prescribed for adultery or gambling. If the husband of an adulterous woman is informed of what is going on, he has the lover's feet squeezed between two splints of wood till the pain grows unendurable and he surrenders all his property as the price for liberation. As with us, there are people who practise swindling.…

Sickness and leprosy

The people of Cambodia often cure themselves of many illnesses by plunging into water and washing the head again and again. Nevertheless, the traveller meets many lepers along the way. Even when these unfortunates sleep and eat among their fellow-countrymen, no protest is made. By some it is said that leprosy is the outcome of climatic conditions. Even one of the sovereigns fell victim to the disease, and so the people do not look on it as a disgrace.…

Agriculture

Generally speaking, three or four crops a year can be counted on, for the entire Cambodian year resembles the fifth and sixth moons of China, and frost and snow are unknown. In this country it rains half the year; the other half has no rain at all. From the fourth to the ninth moon there is rain every afternoon, and the level of the Great Lake may rise seven to eight fathoms. Large trees go under water, with only the tops showing. People living at the water-side leave for the hills. However, from the tenth moon to the third moon of the following year not a drop of rain falls; the Great Lake is navigable only for the smallest craft, and the depth of the water is only three to five feet. The hills are then forsaken. Farmers who have noted when the rice is ripe and the height to which the water then rises in flood, time their sowing according to these findings. Oxen are not used in cultivation. Cambodian ploughs, sickles, and hoes, while bearing some likeness in principle to ours, are made entirely differently. There is, moreover, a certain kind of land where the rice grows naturally, without sowing. When the water is up one fathom, the rice keeps pace in its growth. This, I think, must be a special variety....

The configuration of the land

After crossing the frontier at Chen-p'u, one sees everywhere close-grown thickets of scrub forest; the great estuaries of the Mekong cover hundreds of miles; the heavy shade of old trees and trailing rattan-vines forms a luxuriant cover. Cries of birds and animals weave a tissue of sound. Half-way on one's journey the country opens up suddenly, without a sign of trees. As far as the eye can see there is nothing but an abundance of wild millet. Wild buffaloes, by hundreds and by thousands, graze in groups in this region. This is followed by rising ground covered with bamboo, this too stretching for hundreds of miles. Thorns grow from the joints of this bamboo, and the shoots have a bitter taste. The horizon is bounded on all sides by high mountains....

The sovereign comes forth

I have heard it said that in previous reigns the marks of the King's chariot wheels were never seen outside the palace gates – a precaution against unforeseen violence. The present ruler is the son-in-law of his predecessor, who, devoted as he was to his daughter, gave her the chance to steal the golden sword (of office) and give it to her husband, thus depriving her brother of the succession. This brother strove to stir the soldiery to revolt, but the prince, hearing of this, cut off his brother-in-law's toes and threw him into a dark dungeon. He then caused a splinter of sacred iron to be grafted into his own body, so that any thrust of knife or spear could do him no harm. Once this was brought about, the new King ventured forth. During my stay of over a year in the country I saw him emerge four or five times.

When the King leaves his palace, the procession is headed by the soldiery; then come the flags, the banners, the music. Girls of the palace, three or five hundred in number, gaily dressed, with flowers in their hair and tapers in their hands, are massed together in a separate column. The tapers are lighted even in broad daylight. Then came other girls carrying gold and silver vessels from the palace and a whole galaxy of ornaments, of very special design, the uses of which were strange to me. Then came still more girls, the bodyguard of the palace, holding shields and lances. These, too, were separately aligned. Following them came chariots drawn by goats and horses, all adorned with gold; ministers and princes, mounted on elephants, were preceded by bearers of scarlet parasols, without number. Close behind came the royal wives and concubines, in palanquins and chariots, or mounted on horses or elephants, to whom were assigned at least a hundred parasols mottled with gold. Finally the Sovereign appeared, standing erect on an elephant and holding in his hand the sacred sword. This elephant, his tusks sheathed in gold, was accompanied by bearers of twenty white parasols with golden shafts. All around was a bodyguard of elephants, drawn close together, and still more soldiers for complete protection, marching in close order.

The King was proceeding to a nearby destination where golden palanquins, borne by girls of the palace, were waiting to receive him. For the most part his objective was a little golden pagoda in front of which stood a golden statue of the Buddha. Those who caught a glimpse of the King were expected to kneel and touch the earth with their brows. Failing to perform this obeisance, which is called *sun-pa (sambah)*, they were seized by the masters of ceremonies (marshals) who under no circumstance let them escape.

Every day the King holds two audiences for consideration of affairs of state. No list of agenda is provided. Functionaries and ordinary people who wish to see the Sovereign seat themselves on the ground to await his arrival. In the course of time distant music is heard in the palace, while from outside blasts on conch-shells sound forth as though to welcome the ruler. I have been told that at this point the Sovereign, coming from nearby, contents himself with only one golden palanquin. Two girls of the palace lift up the curtain with their slender fingers and the King, sword in hand, appears standing in the golden window. All present – ministers and commoners – join their hands and touch the earth with their foreheads, lifting up their heads only when the sound of conches has ceased. The Sovereign seats himself at once on a lion's skin, which is an hereditary royal treasure. When the affairs of state have been dealt with the King turns back to the palace, the two girls let fall the curtain, and everyone rises. From all this it is plain to see that these people, though barbarians, know what is due to a Prince.

Zhou Daguan
The Customs of Cambodia, 1993

The Elephant Terrace at Angkor Thom.

Khmer bas-reliefs

In addition to the information gained from inscriptions and travellers' accounts, the bas-reliefs shed light on everyday life in 12th- and 13th-century Cambodia.

In the late 12th century the Khmer did not represent 'everyday life', as we would understand the term today, on the famous bas-reliefs of the Bayon for its own sake. Undoubtedly important activities, such as agriculture and in particular rice growing, are not depicted at all. The reason is because the subject of these compositions was not everyday life. Instead they are always set in a religious context and are only 'historical' in that the history of wars is transposed to the divine realm. As Jean Boisselier has explained so well, the battles that Jayavarman VII and his Khmer and Cham followers waged against their enemies were assimilated with the battles that Indra, the king of the gods, waged against the *asura* demons....

A junk with fishermen; outer southern gallery of the Bayon.

Yet in the Bayon we also find … depicted in a different way from the famous bas-reliefs of Angkor Wat, a series of small scenes showing people in typical everyday occupations. But these little 'genre scenes', generally on the borders and below the main compositions, are only there as props and were probably intended to provide a specific location for the great events depicted above. But these borders clearly reflect the spirit, good nature and individual temperament of the great anonymous artists who worked on this immense sculptural programme. Today it is these subjects (which are not really subjects) that we find most moving, for they literally bring to life the Cambodia of Jayavarman VII.…

Far more so than in Angkor Wat, these very long bas-reliefs – which, sadly, are poorly preserved in several places and sometimes unfinished – provide information on aspects of daily life, nature and human activity in ancient Cambodia. However, certain conventions must be noted. They are apparent, for instance, in the 'scale' images on the rocks that represent mountains and they can also be found in architectural images, which serve simply as frameworks rather than representing real buildings and which sometimes embellish reality. Similarly, the artists were generally less interested in representing individually observed subjects than in concepts, stereotypes; for example, they did not depict one particular ascetic but the ascetic type, in his ideal or even idyllic framework, part natural, part divine.

Albert Le Bonheur
'La vie quotidienne d'après les bas-reliefs du Bayon'
Dossiers Histoire et Archéologie, No. 125, March 1988

Constructing the temple-mountains

How were these colossal monuments built, and how were the stones moved from the quarry to the site, and to their location in the structure? The transportation of these massive blocks of sandstone has been the subject of great speculation, as the stones range in weight from one to eight or ten tons. The blocks were cut and dressed in random sizes at the quarries in Kulen. At that time, it is likely that two pairs of lifting holes were drilled deep into the stones. Bamboo wedges were driven into these holes and vines were lashed between them. When swollen with water, the wedges would grip the stones tightly. The stones were probably lifted by elephant onto bamboo barges and floated down the rivers and waterways to the building sites, where, using the same system, they were lifted and stacked into the new structure. A series of ramps, presumably, enabled elephants to haul the stones close to the site. The stone would later be raised into position with something similar to a block and tackle.

Prior to stacking, wafer-thin joints between the stones were engineered by rubbing or abrading the stones, one against the other, until there was an exact match of the stones' faces. This process is depicted in one of the … [inner gallery] bas-reliefs on the west side of the Bayon…. Afterward the stones were laid dry, ready for rough shaping by masons, whether as doors, windows, or decorative niches, or as part of a bas-relief. Ultimately, they received the fine hand of the sculptors to finish the detailed decoration. Often the lifting holes are still visible, and it appears that in several temples the holes were later disguised with stucco. It is hard to imagine how some of the ashlar stone

An important person, possibly the king, lies prostrate before a statue of Vishnu, who wears the finery of the time; inner southern gallery of the Bayon (above).

A buffalo, tied to a tree, is prepared for sacrifice before a battle; outer eastern gallery of the Bayon (above). These sacrifices, common until recently, were supposed to bring good luck.

walling with its complicated jointing pattern was achieved. The stones themselves are fitted together like patchwork: no two stones are alike nor are they laid in regular courses, so the walls have the appearance of marquetry or a giant jigsaw puzzle, with joints so tight they are almost invisible. In many places special wedge-shaped keystones were driven in to tighten the joints.

Once the stones had been stacked, the process of decorating the temple began by a team of masons who blocked out the detail. Finally, the panels were finished by a highly skilled group of sculptors. A similar process, probably involving several more stages, was no doubt used to design and carve the awe-inspiring bas-reliefs at the Bayon and Angkor Wat.

It is certain that this process was followed, as there are examples everywhere of uncompleted work. In particular at the Bayon, many of the

During major festivals jugglers performed for the entertainment of all the people; outer northern gallery of the Bayon. The upper register of this bas-relief was never carved.

with the shaping and carving of the structures in situ. Windows were cut, door jambs prepared in the wall slab, architraves shaped, niches carved, pilasters hewn, and, later, the decorative geometric and floral patterns were added. The more exacting task of sculpting the facade then followed. The master carver engraved an overall design onto the facade; he was followed

upper registers of bas-reliefs have been left unfinished.... The construction of the Khmer temple-mountains was a mammoth undertaking....

John Sanday
'The Triumphs and Perils of Khmer Architecture' in Helen Ibbitson Jessup and Thierry Zéphir (eds.), *Sculpture of Angkor and Ancient Cambodia: Millennium of Glory*, 1997

An uncertain legacy: the Khmer paradox

Bernard-Philippe Groslier was the last French curator of the site of Angkor. Here he considers both the greatness of ancient Cambodian civilization and the reasons for its limited influence.

Face tower from the Bayon.

The significance of the Khmer civilization

Our knowledge of Khmer civilization is far from complete: many surprises are in store, too many problems await detailed study. We can at least pronounce judgment on the period from the ninth to the twelfth centuries which witnessed the pre-eminence of Angkor. The chronological and historical framework is based on solid foundations; we are familiar with the principal buildings and can follow the course of their evolution. Though our interpretation of the facts is still far from certain, we may without undue risk attempt to draw certain conclusions of general application.

The Khmer civilization was the most important, the most brilliant and original in ancient Indo-China. Although classification by order of merit is a somewhat puerile historical pastime, it can also be regarded as one of the greatest, together with that of Indonesia, in the whole of Indianized Asia.

The brilliant achievements of ancient Cambodia were due primarily to the country's wealth of natural resources. No other country of the peninsula could boast of such an unbroken extent of fertile and well-watered land. Cambodia, being a strictly defined and admirably situated geographical unit, was the cradle of a powerful and gifted race. The people were left in peace throughout ten centuries, without any outside interference....

But neither a favourable environment nor limitless resources nor years of peace would have sufficed without the spiritual contribution of India. India was the spark that fired the blaze. A strongly centralized society gradually grew up round the king, the god on earth, who guaranteed its spiritual and material existence. It was to this concentration of power as well as to her flourishing economy that Cambodia owed her unrivalled fame. We are reminded, though on a more modest scale, of the Roman Empire united by the cult of Caesar, or better still of the Chinese Empire, itself also the product of the exploitation of the soil and of a religion both of which centred on the person of the Emperor. In this respect Cambodia sometimes even surpassed her Indian teachers....

On the other hand, we must not be led by its undeniable brilliance to bestow unqualified praise on Khmer civilization. It contained within itself the seeds of its own destruction. An excessive and too exclusive inflation of the royal power produced a kind of hypertrophy which exhausted the nation beyond hope of recovery. The country was milked dry for the sole benefit of the king. Religion and art alike were dedicated to his service. Our judgment may perhaps be warped owing to the disappearance of all secular writings and of an incalculable number of works of art. But there is no evidence of any healthy philosophy developing outside the cult of the king-god, after whose disappearance there was in any case nothing capable of regenerating the nation. In such a closed society nothing was left to pin one's faith on – except Buddhism, a religion of total renunciation.

For this reason Khmer culture was not only doomed to perish sooner or later, but was incapable of spreading. It is obvious that it was the germ of the civilizations of Siam and Laos, and had a profound influence on the Chams. But the sole reason for this was that these countries were more or less under Khmer domination, deriving from a related racial stock and living under

similar conditions. Khmer civilization was valid in the environment and specific circumstances from which it emerged, but it could not be reproduced in other times and places. Cambodia must consequently be classed with those cultures which, splendid though they may be, have never, like Egypt, Japan and the Empire of the Incas, transcended their geographical and ethnical frontiers. There have, as we know, been centres of civilization, perhaps of less brilliant achievement, which have nevertheless proved models of inspiration to other lands: such for example as Greece, Israel, Iran, Rome, China and India – 'countries greater than themselves', as René Grousset liked to call them.

It is perhaps worth while attempting to discover the reason why some civilizations are like beautiful but barren trees, while others are laden with blossom and fruit. The former, in our opinion, are doomed because they are incapable of evolving a philosophy of man and his destiny. In this field ancient Cambodia was satisfied with what India gave her, and even so was content to remain second best. In spite of the extraordinary development of the State in Cambodia, she appears never to have formulated any theory of power or public welfare such as was bequeathed to all Europe by Rome and to the Far East by China. In Cambodia there was no society, nothing but an undefined juxtaposition of elementary and undifferentiated cells. There were no classes, none of those intermediate and unstable structures which alone provide any possibility of evolution. There was nothing but a vast anonymous proletariat, with a head which may have been wonderful but was, after all, severed from the body. It was a polypous society, a hive incapable of self-reproduction other than by swarming, doomed inexorably to die, as soon as the mother-cell, the queen, is destroyed.

Great initial gifts, long-maintained prosperity, and certainly a wonderful achievement. Yet nothing of all this survives but a vague memory. Such, no doubt, is the fate of all greatness divorced from love. Nor must it be forgotten that the record of the Khmers survives only because our own humanism, faithful to its proper task, has been at pains to exhume it and bring it back to life almost in spite of itself.

Moreover it is only a portion of that past that has any interest for us today. The history of the Khmers has its place, like any other human fact, in the field of general knowledge. The evolution of Khmer society is a fruitful theme for the consideration of the sociologist. Yet neither is of primary importance,

because both lie outside the main streams of universal history, and neither has left any offspring. The undying glory and unique legacy of ancient Cambodia are to be found in the wonderful monuments which stand sentinel in Angkor.

A legacy from the past: Khmer art

…It would be easy to point to a more masterly architecture, a more remarkable sculpture, a more logical decoration. Among the other works of art produced in Asia itself there are many more meaningful and more sympathetic. The art of Angkor, like its culture, was not a source of universal inspiration. In saying this we may be doing an injustice to the fine productions of medieval Cambodia or Siam, of which we know so little but which have sometimes proved worthy successors to the Angkor traditions. But it must be admitted that we cannot

The temple-mountain of Ta Keo.

speak of a Khmer aesthetic, or cannot at any rate say that it was one of those discoveries which become a permanent part of human experience.

It may be agreed that the art of Angkor was instinctive, lacking in restraint and too often prosaic, and that it left no heirs. Nevertheless Angkor remains a unique ensemble, equally fascinating to the newcomer and to the scholar who has spent years in its study. I am inclined to believe that its secret is to be found in that word 'ensemble'. Taken in detail Khmer art is always a little disappointing. But its size is unsurpassable, the harmony of these enormous structures, the feeling of what may be called urbanism. The temple-mountain symbolizes a whole universe, and owes its grandeur to the very loftiness of its aim. Standing as it does in the centre of the city it makes its effect by its wonderful perspectives of light and shade. From the mind that conceived it, it derives its diagrammatic effect and its symbolic power. The faith that raised its stones has imprinted on them the touching beauty of the human face. And because it was constructed out of space and time, it still dominates the one and has defied the other, lifting its temples in a perpetual gesture against the sky.

The regal majesty and calm repose of Angkor Wat; the troubled message of the Bayon with its hundred faces…. Fully to express them we need something more than words, something better than pictures: we need to add the dawn breaking over the forest, the sun's ray suddenly piercing the clouds – and the silence….

Rare breezes and shifting lights; a heavy coolness; indefinable scents; immobility rather than death, and repose rather than sadness. All these

Female divinity in the Angkor Wat style (first half of 12th century). Overleaf: footsoldiers from Suryavarman II's army.

make up the beauty of the stones of Angkor and the memory of the men who wrought them.

Bernard-Philippe Groslier
Angkor: Art and Civilization,
translated by Eric Ernshaw Smith, 1966

FURTHER READING

ART AND ARCHAEOLOGY

Boisselier, Jean, *Le Cambodge*, 1966
— *La Statuaire khmère et son évolution*, 1955
— *Trends in Khmer Art*, 1989
Finot, Louis, Victor Goloubew and George Coedès, *Le Temple d'Angkor Vat*, 1927–32
Giteau, Madeleine, *Iconographie du Cambodge post-angkorien*, 1975
— *Khmer Sculpture and the Angkor Civilization*, trans. Diana Imber, 1965
Glaize, Maurice, *Les Monuments du groupe d'Angkor*, 1993
Groslier, Bernard-Philippe, *Indochina: Art in the Melting Pot of Races*, trans. George Lawrence, 1962
Groslier, Bernard-Philippe, *Angkor: Art and Civilization*, trans. Eric Ernshaw Smith, 1966
Lunet de La Jonquière, Etienne E., *Inventaire descriptif des monuments du Cambodge*, 1902–11
Parmentier, Henri, *L'Art khmer classique*, 1939
— *L'Art khmer primitif*, 1927
Stern, Philippe, *Les Monuments khmers du style du Bayon et Jayavarman VII*, 1965

HISTORY AND RELIGION

Bhattacharya, Kamaleswar, *Les Religions brahmaniques dans l'ancien Cambodge*, 1961

Boisselier, Jean, *The Wisdom of the Buddha*, 1993
Coedès, George, *Angkor, An Introduction*, trans. Emily Floyd Gardiner, 1963
— *The Indianized States of Southeast Asia*, trans. S.B. Cowing, 1971
— *The Making of South East Asia*, trans. H. M. Wright, 1966
Groslier, Bernard-Philippe, *Angkor et le Cambodge au XVIe siècle d'après les sources portugaises et espagnoles*, 1958
Tarling, Nicholas (ed.), *The Cambridge History of Southeast Asia*, 1992
Zhou Daguan, *The Customs of Cambodia*, 1993

RECENT WORKS

Ang, Choulean, Eric Prenowitz, Ashley Thompson, *Angkor: Past, Present and Future*, 1996
Dagens, Bruno, *Angkor: Heart of an Asian Empire*, 1995
Girard-Geslan, Maud, Thierry Zéphir, et al., *Art of Southeast Asia*, 1998
Jacques, Claude, and René Dumont, *Angkor*, 1990
Jessup, Helen Ibbitson, and Thierry Zéphir (eds.), *Sculpture of Angkor and Ancient Cambodia: Millennium of Glory*, 1997
Le Bonheur, Albert, *Cambodge, Angkor, Temples en péril*, 1989
— *Of Gods, Kings and Men, Bas-reliefs of Angkor Wat and Bayon*, 1995

LIST OF ILLUSTRATIONS

The following abbreviations have been used:
a above; *b* below; *c* centre; *l* left; *r* right.
MG Musée National des Arts Asiatiques Guimet, Paris. NMC National Museum of Cambodia, Phnom Penh.

COVER

OPENING

CHAPTER 1

CHAPTER 2

CHAPTER 3

DOCUMENTS

INDEX

NOTE ON TRANSCRIPTION AND PRONUNCIATION

For the sake of clarity a simplified transcription of Sanskrit has been used. Generally every letter is pronounced in both Sanskrit and Khmer.

ACKNOWLEDGMENTS

The author wishes to thank Anne de Margerie, director of the publications department of the Réunion des Musées Nationaux; Irène Bizot, general administrator of the Réunion des Musées Nationaux; Jean-François Jarrige, curator general of the Musée National des Arts Asiatiques Guimet; Helen Ibbitson Jessup, guest curator of the National Gallery of Art, Washington, D. C.; John Gollings, many of whose photographs appear in this volume; Pich Keo, Cambodian minister for culture and art; Ang Choulean, lecturer at the faculty of archaeology, Phnom Penh.

The publishers also thank Marie-Claude Bianchini, editor at the Réunion des Musées Nationaux, and the entire 'Angkor' team of the Ecole Française d'Extrême-Orient.

PHOTO CREDITS

TEXT CREDITS

(pp. 98–9) George Coèdes, *The Indianized States of Southeast Asia*, translated by S. B. Cowing, 1971; reprinted by permission of University of Hawaii Press, Honolulu. (pp. 111–3) Quoted from 'The Triumphs and Perils of Khmer Architecture' by John Sanday, in *Sculpture of Angkor and Ancient Cambodia: Millennium of Glory*, copyright National Gallery of Art, Washington, D. C., 1997, pages 87 and 88; reprinted by permission of the National Gallery of Art, Washington, D. C.

Thierry Zéphir,
researcher at the Musée Guimet, organized the
exhibition 'Angkor et dix siècles d'art khmer',
which for the first time brought together the
masterpieces of ancient Cambodian sculpture
from the Musée Guimet in Paris and the
National Museum of Cambodia, Phnom Penh.
A former student of Albert Le Bonheur,
Thierry Zéphir is a graduate of the
Ecole du Louvre, where he now teaches.
His main field of research is the art
and techniques of Khmer bronzes.

To Giuliocesare

Translated from the French by Francisca Garvie

For Harry N. Abrams, Inc.
Eve Sinaiko, editorial
Julio Bravo, cover design

Library of Congress Cataloging-in-Publication Data

Zéphir, Thierry.
    [Empire des rois Khmers. English]
    Khmer, the lost empire of Cambodia / Thierry Zéphir.
        p.   cm. — (Discoveries)
    Includes index.
    ISBN 0–8109–2853–1 (paperback)
    1. Cambodia—History—800–1444.   I. Title.   II. Series:
Discoveries (New York, N.Y.)
DS554.62.Z4713 1998
959.6'.03—dc21   97–42419

Copyright © 1997 Gallimard/RMN

English translation copyright © 1998 Thames and Hudson Ltd., London

Published in 1998 by Harry N. Abrams, Inc., New York

Printed and bound in Italy by Editoriale Libraria, Trieste